D1592665

GRAPHIC DESIGN IN ARCHITECTURE

DESIGN MEDIA PUBLISHING LIMITED

CONTENTS >>

186 OFFICE >>   # 262 CULTURE & SPORT >>

PERFACE >>

Not long ago, graphic design in architecture was only thought of as putting up signs to a building after it was designed and mostly built. It was a necessity, but was mostly considered as a visual distraction from the overall design statement.

Then, innovative designers and firms such as Masimo Vignelli, Chermayeff & Geismar, John Follis and the GNU Group designed a number of groundbreaking projects, which began the conversation that graphics could be an important part of the overall architectural design statement.

Those who ventured into this new field were from diverse backgrounds including graphic design, architecture, interior design, industrial design, fashion design and others. This spoke to the wide variety of skills needed for this form of design, but also suggested that environmental graphics could be approached from a number of starting points.

Now, graphic design is considered a key element in the overall success in the design of commercial architecture. As urban areas become more populated, high quality environmental graphics are very important in differentiating one office building from another, in suggesting a feeling of quality or progressiveness to clients, of reinforcing a new brand direction, or in helping you to make it to your flight on time.

Graphic designers are brought into project in earlier stages of design, with graphics often considered a significant part of the basic design approach. Many architects now embrace graphics in the conceptualisation of buildings and spaces, acknowledging their important role in the expression of a design, and as a key element in tying together the function of their buildings with the humans that will inhabit them.

The public, consumers and workers understand the importance of graphics in navigating complex spaces, enlivening daily experiences, and making architecture more accessible to those with disabilities or special needs. The explosion of graphic design in the media has made us all much more knowledgeable and sophisticated consumers of this visual data, and requires that environmental graphics communicate the right message on a number of levels.

Environmental graphics are expected to be functional, visible, unique, manageable and hopefully to make our life easier and more enjoyable. They can do the important task of breaking down complexity into small bites, or to lend visual richness to an otherwise uninspiring space. They can provide information that can give new perspective and understanding, and can ease people's minds in stressful situations. They can stimulate a feeling of discovery and experiencing things in a new way. They can bring focus to people's intellects and emotions, deepening understanding, and connecting with others.

As the world becomes more mobile, graphics need to be more carefully considered, as the audience for these visual communications is becoming much more diverse. Potential cultural issues need to be accounted for in the potential viewing audiences of these graphics, as colours, forms and other visual aspects are often as large of a communication factor as the words contained on the signs.

Also, environmental graphics can be just signs, and we need signs. We need to know that is a one-way street, that an alarm will go off if we go out that door, that this is a wheelchair accessible entrance, that procedures need to be followed at security checkpoints and that this is our seat at a sporting event. But even these mundane elements, that we mostly perceive as important visual clutter, can become environmental graphics, when the designers take the time to consider all of the needs of those who will use their buildings. All of the potential audiences of this information need to be considered, from those that work in the space every day, to those that are visiting for the first time. Flexibility is important in many types of sign elements, as informational needs change as the functions that buildings support evolve.

Graphics for architecture need to be designed with careful consideration, as the product of this design is much more permanent in nature than in other areas of graphic design. Graphic objects that are initially a spectacular landmark can become visual blight over time if too much emphasis is placed on the expression of a design concept of the moment. This of course is an important consideration in the larger picture of architectural design also, so project design teams must always stay focused on both how the objects they design will look and function in 10 years, not just at the grand opening. This requirement varies depending on the type of architecture, as retail venues look to visually refresh their shopping centres frequently, while public buildings need to stand the test of time.

All of these factors make graphics in architecture a challenging and constantly evolving field, and one that I am happy to be a part of. The speed of this evolution requires one to keep up with trends in technology, construction, communications, fashion and culture, as some or all of these can provide important insites that lead to the right design solution for a project.

Graphic Design in Architecture provides an extensive current snapshot of the range of work being done in this vital field of design, by a number of today's leading design firms. We hope that you enjoy this book and that it inspires you to further investigate the great work being done in this field.

Tom Donnelly
GNU Group

The Principles of Commercial Wayfinding and Environmental Graphic Design

In any building, especially public spaces, people need continual "direction" so they can find the way to their destination. The same is true for outdoor spaces such as pedestrian malls, zoological parks – even roadways.

The science of the design, manufacture and installation of these "sensory cues" is called wayfinding, and it involves a discipline called "environmental graphic design".

Effective signage design and signage placement is essential for the success of any commercial project. User-friendly navigational systems must provide simple, logical guidance for users. Ideally, these systems will also integrate seamlessly with the brand and with the architectural elements, and feel of the space.

Functional wayfinding systems work in conjunction with architectural landmarks. For example, major entrance areas in shopping centres and hotels frequently have prominent names, colours, materials, art and/or sculptural elements, providing location cues that support wayfinding.

Usually, the simplest and most functional wayfinding systems are the result of a great deal of planning on the part of experienced environmental graphic designers and wayfinding experts.

Exterior signage is typically the most visible component of a wayfinding project, especially in an area with both vehicular and pedestrian traffic. It's essential that this signage be minimal, yet very clear, so as to guide visitors safely into the environment at critical decision points. Such signage should also be memorable, should complement the surrounding architecture, and should support the brand.

Again, thinking and planning for each individual sign and its placement is critical before the actual design of the signage can be completed. It's very important to the visitor experience – and for safety – that all exterior signs provide users with a clear, confident navigation path.

Once inside a facility, even more specific destination information must be provided. As with exterior wayfinding, a hierarchy of signage is essential to interior wayfinding. Interior sign type categories include building, lobby, floor identification, directory and directional signage and regulatory signage.

Retail storefronts are the final destination in shopping centres or at remote sites. The signage for a storefront is a small part of the overall fascia design, which includes a combination of architectural materials and display windows intended to catch the potential shoppers' attention. Consistency in retail storefront design and signage is intended to provide consistent branding for multiple or chain stores. Effective signage enables the shopper to quickly identify the brand and feel comfortable and familiar with each location.

A key element of interior signage is the "directory sign", which provides even more details about the space as a visitor walks up to the sign. These signs need to be located close to entrances and at major decision points throughout the space. Successful directory signage is based on the designer's ability to depict complex elements of an environment in a simple, universally-understandable manner. Directory signs and "maps" should be based on the viewer's orientation within a space, rather than a "compass north" orientation, which can be confusing to first time visitors.

More use is being made these days of international pictograms, multi-lingual elements and universally-familiar images on signs. These elements can minimise clutter on maps and signs while effectively communicating key public destinations such as restrooms, elevators, information kiosks and stairs.

Experienced wayfinding and environmental graphic design professionals typically undertake a multi-step process in order to deliver a successful project.

Step one involves analysis and master-planning including orientation meetings, regulatory rules, terminology, traffic patterns, etc. Step two includes schematic design and design documentation, location plans, message schedules, budgeting and sample work. Step three involves construction documentation, and the final step is construction administration and supervision.

In summary, environmental graphic and wayfinding design is a very involved process requiring a great deal of thought, teamwork, research, planning and a knowledge of branding.

Richard Lang
Visual Communications, Inc

World Square Car Park >>

BrandCulture were intent on turning this around with the World Square Car Park, by creating a welcoming environment that was simple to navigate and easy to understand. Located in the heart of Sydney's CBD, the World Square Car Park is an amalgamation of several car parks situated under the new developments that make up the largest multi-functional complex in Australia. The research showed that car parks were often quite dangerous and with poor identification of exits and emergency equipment. The designers applied innovative wayfinding principles of cognitive mapping and circulatory navigation combined with integrated and intuitive design for the best outcome. The solution to the challenge for pedestrians came through establishing two lines of sight: the first visible from motor vehicles, using full height icons, giant type and bold colours; and the second from the more elevated position of a pedestrian standing. This experiential factor became a differentiator between this car park and so many others around the globe. Meanwhile, every graphic element, colour placement and typography was considered for its ability to communicate information concisely and consistently. Playful, super-scaled level numbers and icon graphics were combined with blocks of bright, punchy and memorable colours to help orient drivers and pedestrians from the moment they arrive at World Square.

Design Agency:
BrandCulture
Creative Director:
Stephen Minning
Design Director:
Antonijo Bacic
Photography:
Kris Baum
Stephen Minning
Client:
World Square
Location:
Sydney, Australia
Date:
2008

Hill
Country
Galleria >>

The Hill Country Galleria is a mixed-use lifestyle centre on the edge of Austin.The client commissioned RTKL for graphics and signage that would be straightforward and utilitarian and provide much-needed navigation. The design team saw an opportunity to take the assignment one step further and created a solution that was functional and cost effective but that also greatly contributed to the overall sense of place and customer experience.The resulting programme reflects local Austin character without being overly thematic. Materials and details imitate the rolling countryside and feature local white limestone, rusted steel faux finishes, exposed bolts, and an agrarian-based colour palette. The logo, inspired by traditional ranch brands, is simple, yet powerful, leaving a distinguished mark throughout the entire environment. Directional markers, parking signs and pedestrian directories form a space that feels comfortable and honest yet unique in character.

Design Agency:
RTKL Associates Inc.
Photography:
Jason Koenig
Client:
Opus West Corporation
Location:
Bee Cave, Texas,USA
Date:
2008

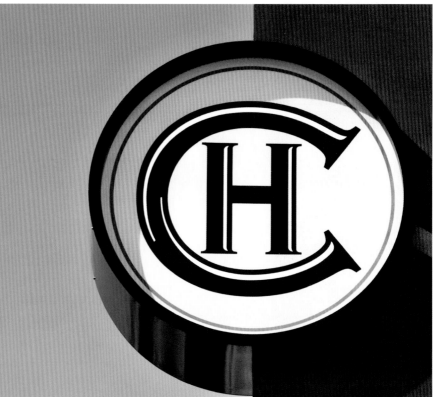

Bellevue
Square
Renovation >>

Bellevue Square is a family-owned but nationally known retail destination. RTKL was hired to renovate Bellevue Square with the intent of upgrading its finishes to match the design quality of a recent mall expansion and of adjacent new mixed-use projects developed by the mall's ownership. A restrained palette of wood and glass was strategically added to complement existing exposed concrete columns and bulkheads, transforming an industrial space into industrial chic. New lighting rectifies long-standing issues with dark areas, mostly through the installation of indirect sources in coves and pockets. Great attention was paid to maintaining the simplicity and integrity of the original design. RTKL is working with the local architectural firm who first designed Bellevue Square in the 1970s to ensure that the transformed spaces are embraced by the long-standing and loyal clientele of Bellevue Square.

Design Agency:
RTKL Associates Inc.
Photography:
David Whitcomb
Client:
Bellevue Square
Location:
USA
Date:
2009

Third Floor ↑

KIDS' COVE

Bellevue Chamber of Commerce

Restrooms

GYMBOREE. PLAY & MUSIC

Metropolis Mall >>

Prominently located on a major highway encircling Moscow, Metropolis represents a new generation of commercial development for a burgeoning region of the city. The 315,000-square-metre retail and office development had two goals – introducing a modern mixed-use environment that supports around-the-clock activity while creating a sophisticated space that fits into the local setting.

Inspired by the energy of city centres, the design of Metropolis mimics an open-air street scene. Retail corridors that resemble shopping boulevards employ colours, patterns and finishes to transform individual storefronts into dynamic façades. Various architecture details continue the aesthetic of an outdoor lifestyle centre including a grand plaza and garden that form a junction between the retail component and three office buildings. With close proximity to public transportation, Metropolis is a celebrated extension of downtown Moscow.

Design Agency:
RTKL Associates Inc.
Photography:
David Whitcomb
Client:
Capital Partners
Location:
Moscow, Russia
Date:
2009

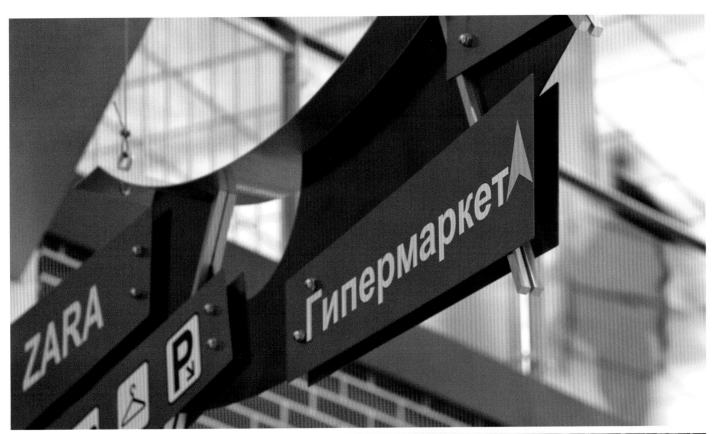

360°
Mall >>

Design Agency:
RTKL Associates Inc.
Photography:
Mitch Duncan
Client:
Tamdeen
Location:
Kuwait City, Kuwait
Date:
2009

While retail developers and designers around the world strive to create places that encourage visitors to linger and to return, nowhere is this task more challenging than in the Middle East, where the harsh desert climate keeps residents indoors for the majority of the year. For the design of 360° Mall, RTKL was commissioned to create a hub of retail, entertainment, and leisure offerings that would act as an indoor civic centre and an extension of everyday living where residents and tourists can gather to socialise and shop.

The design of the 130,000-square-metre centre, which is located at the intersection of two major highways, is configured as a journey that highlights the natural and cultural features of its location. The name 360° guides all elements of the scheme and references organic and manmade symbols, from the rotation of the Earth to the needle on a compass, an important reference to the historic Arabic art of navigation. The distinctive rounded exterior comprises a carved limestone façade surrounded by lush landscaping and water features. Inside, visitors progress through a main entry and into a techno hub, a versatile space designed to showcase information about the centre and its sponsors. The retail diagram unfolds in two opposing concourses, "day journey" and "night journey". The design elements in each concourse – from lighting to graphics to interior architecture – respond to the qualities implied by "day" and "night". At the intersection of the corridors, a three-level crescent-shaped atrium features bronze screens that reinterpret traditional Arabic patterns.

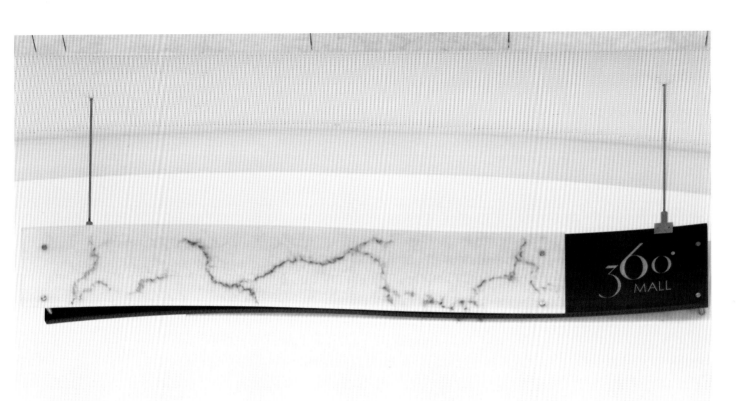

Alexa
Shopping
Centre >>

In the heart of the former Soviet territory in East Berlin, RTKL was commissioned to contribute to the redevelopment of Alexanderplatz, a historic central plaza at the heart of Berlin cultural life in the pre-WW2 era. The resulting design for "Alexa", a mixed-use retail and entertainment centre, uses a daring, sophisticated 1920s woman as its fictional muse to evoke the area's rich artistic past.

The interior architecture and layout of Alexa are reflective of its exterior, designed to establish the development as the centrepiece of the square. The highest floor of the building, topped off on two sides with a plated gold "Alexa" logo, contains a cineplex, bowling alley, and state-of-the-art health club. The lower floors are a stimulating mix of natural light and vibrant colours, populated with a variety of specialty retail and dining options. Throughout the building are large-scale art-deco murals and bold, freestanding sculptures. Encased by glass ceilings and wide, sweeping hallways, the artistic mood of the interior calls to mind the centre's heyday while establishing its promising future.

Design Agency:
RTKL Associates Inc.
Photography:
David Whitcomb
Client:
Alexa Shopping Centre
Location:
Berlin, Germany
Date:
2007

Ingelsta
Shopping
Centre >>

The concept was based on the idea "Communication to the big and little ", which was executed on all levels. The graphic identity has, for example, two symbols, a large and small dot. As well, all signs were designed to communicate in duplicate: one message at adult level and one at eye-level for children. The mascot "Inge" was created, and, along with his companion characters, placed out in the environment and printed material. The kids even got their own little toilet, their own café tables and even their own little menu with mini-cinnamon buns.

Design Agency:
BVD
Designer:
Carin Blidholm Svensson
Creative Director:
Kina Gisenfeld Herner
Client:
Eurocommercial Properties
Location:
Stockholm, Sweden
Date:
2008

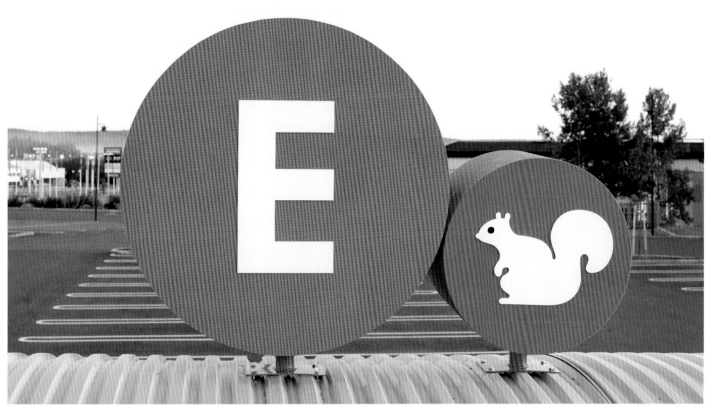

Öppettider
Mån–tor 14–19
Fre 12–19
Lör–sön 12–18.30

→

Här kan du som är 3–8 år leka och
få nya kompisar. Du checkar in hos
våra lekledare med namn och någon
vuxens mobilnummer. Maximal lektid
är en timme. Kom så sätter vi igång!

Ingvar

Ingrid

Ticket
Shop >>

In collaboration with Koncept Arkitekter, BVD created the new shop concept, based on the idea of "that special buzz". That particular feeling comes when you are just about to embark on a trip. Typography and graphic symbols are similar to those found at airports. The red colour has been made brighter and livelier. Texts and pictures have been given a new tone, which helps to increase the "buzz". The new desks reduce the distance between clients and sales staff and increase the feeling of openness and personal contact.

Design Agency:
BVD
Designer:
Carin Blidholm Svensson
Creative Director:
Rikard Ahlberg
Art Director:
Bengt Anderung
Client:
Ticket Privatresor AB
Location:
Stockholm, Sweden
Date:
2009

Pressbyrån Retail Store >>

BVD was comissioned to design Reitan Servicehandel AB Retail Store's concept, communication and signage system, interior design, both in Pressbyrån Sweden and Narvesen Norway in 2007.

The previous retail concept from 2002 worked poorly, especially in the areas of communication, function, and quality. Pressbyrån and Narvesen were in need of a concept that could be used in both chains, while at the same time keeping the distinctiveness and identity of each brand.

Flexibility and scalability were priorities, as were keeping down construction and operation costs. Due to increased competition, Pressbyrån and Narvesen needed to strengthen their respective brands.

BVD created a modern hub with everything that the modern big citizens need. The intention was to turn Pressbyrån into a destination, rather than an institution

Design Agency:
BVD
Designer:
Carin Blidholm Svensson
Creative Director:
Rikard Ahlberg
Art Director:
Johan Andersson
Client:
Reitan Servicehandel AB
Location:
Stockholm, Sweden
Date:
2007

tjänster

Hitta rätt bland våra tjänster!

spel
Prova någon av våra lotter.

nöjen
Surfa på våra datorer, hyr de senaste dvd-filmerna eller ge bort ett presentkort från SF bio.

resor
Köp eller hämta ut din SJ-biljett här. För den lokala resan säljer vi SL-kort.

mobil
Ladda din mobil med något av våra kontantkort, eller ring billigt utomlands med internationellt telefonkort.

pengar
Läs in plusgirot, betala trängselskatt eller skicka pengar på ett säkert sätt.

brev
Vi har frimärken och kuvert i kassan. Vykort hittar du i butiken.

godis

kaffe

pocket

Stads-
schouwburg
Haarlem
Theatre >>

Thonik examines for the house style of the Stadsschouwburg Haarlem how a flexible graphical image can provide a strong identity for the theatre. The studio designed a house style in which notions of glamour, light, glare and shade form the starting point. The mosaics in the interior form the basics for this design. The result is a specific font that can be used as text, image and logo. A text or logo of the Stadsschouwburg Haarlem are never the same, they are literally always lit from different sides. Besides the new identity Thonik also designed the signage of the building and together with fashion designer Alexander van Slobbe the clothes of the staff.

Design Agency:
Thonik
Client:
Stadsschouwburg Haarlem
Location:
Haarlem, The Netherlands
Date:
2009

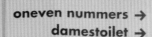

oneven nummers →
damestoilet →

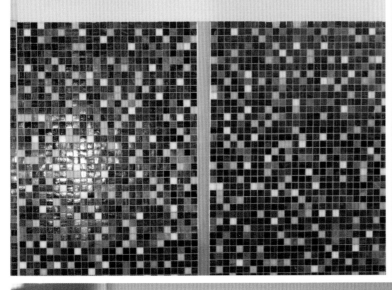

zaal

2e
balkon

↑ balkon 2
↑ torenfoyer

spiegel
foyer

Annenberg
Community
Beach
House >>

The Annenberg Community Beach House at Santa Monica State Beach is a public facility with club-like amenities located on five acres of oceanfront property. It sits on a site which was once the opulent private estate that newspaper magnate William Randolph Hearst purchased for his movie star paramour Marion Davies. Later, the property became the Sand & Sea Club, a limited-membership beach club. Although only the guest cottage and pool remain from the original structures, an extensive ten-year restoration resulted in new beach recreation areas, tennis and volleyball courts, snack bar, meeting and event rooms. AdamsMorioka created the identity, the wayfinding, ADA, and informational signage system for the Beach House.

AdamsMorioka worked with The City of Santa Monica, the Annenberg Foundation, who provided an endowment for the facility, and Frederick Fisher Partners, Architects on the project. Taking cues from the original Hearst architect, Julia Morgan's work, AdamsMorioka developed a vibrant colour palette and kinetic system of interchangeable beach-inspired icons that anchor the identity. The design revolves around the idea of stripes, which echo the verticality of the new freestanding pool house column structures as well as the many palm trees that surround the property.

Design Agency:
AdamsMorioka, Inc.
Client:
The City of Santa Monica
California State Parks
The Annenberg Foundation
Location:
USA
Date:
2008

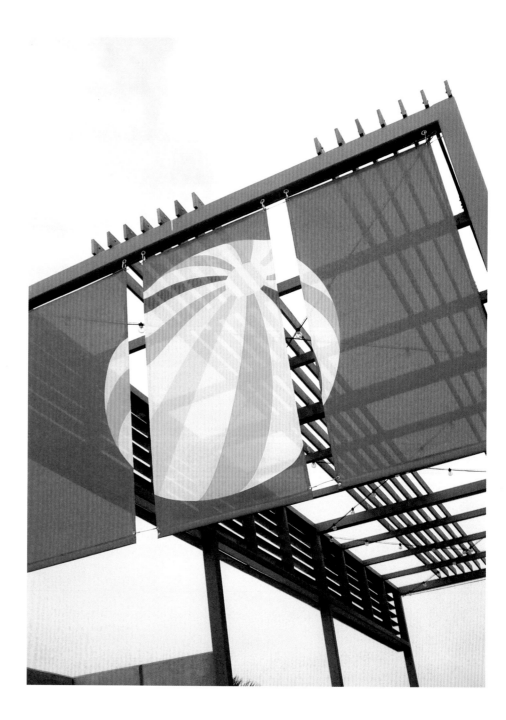

POOL RULES

For the safety and enjoyment of all pool guests:

- Swimmers must shower before entering the water
- Swim suits or equivalent must be worn in the water
- Children under age 12 must be accompanied and supervised by an adult at all times
- Children under age 8 and under 4' in height must be accompanied by an adult in the water at all times
- Children requiring diapers must wear a swim diaper in the water

POOL RULES

The following are prohibited:

- Running, rough play, pushing or dunking of others
- Bikes, scooters, skates, skateboards
- Glass containers
- Masks, fins or snorkels during recreational swim
- Toys in the water, unless distributed by Beach House staff
- Flotation devices (except Coast Guard approved lifejackets)

Guests must abide by the decision of Beach House staff regarding the interpretation of any rules governing the use of this facility. Any behavior or activity determined by the staff to be unsafe, hazardous, inappropriate or a violation of the rules is prohibited.

MAXIMUM OCCUPANCY 113

WARNING: NO LIFEGUARD ON DUTY

Children under the age of 14 should not use pool without an adult in attendance.

NO DIVING ALLOWED

IN CASE OF EMERGENCY CALL 911

ARTIFICIAL RESPIRATION

1. Call 911
2. Tilt head, lift chin, check breathing
3. Give two breaths
4. Position hands on the center of chest
5. Firmly push down 2 inches on the chest 30 times
6. Continue with 2 breaths and 30 pumps until help arrives

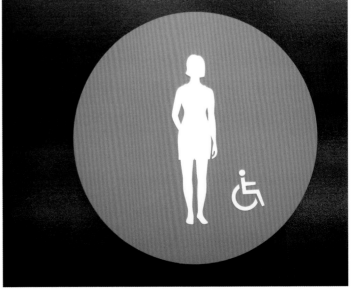

Migros DO IT + GARDEN Retail Chain >>

This project is a development of a wayfinding system for Migros DO IT + GARDEN to get on the shortest way to the product. One of the fundamental measures in the context of the repositioning of retail space by DO IT + GARDEN Migros is the fast, simple and clear guidance for the customer with verbal and illustrative elements (name and Pictogram) as well as colours. The designers assume that in future, the DO IT + GARDEN must make do with fewer staff. This means that customers are increasingly dependent on information support. Development of a pictogram signage system for the Migros DO IT + GARDEN, which is used nationwide.

Design Agency:
AdamsMorioka, Inc.
Client:
Migros Do It+Garden
Location:
Switzerland
Date:
2009

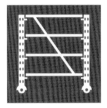

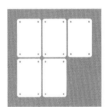

  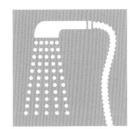  

Moskau
Orientation
System >>

In 1964, in East Germany a restaurant opened with the name "Café Moskau" in the owned building of the "Volk" trade organisation. Especially the transparency and lightness of the architecture through the open atrium structure is unique. Moniteurs developed the corporate design and the signage system for Moskau, which now offers space for events, conferences, exhibitions and marketing-events to the ewerk GmbH. The design portrays light, the universe and planetary constellation – for the grand opening ceremony, an original sized sputnik, a present from the former ambassador to the USSR, was installed.

Design Agency:
Moniteurs GmbH
Designer:
Heike Nehl
Anne von Borries
Maximilian Mittermeier
Client:
Moskau GmbH
Location:
Germany
Date:
2009

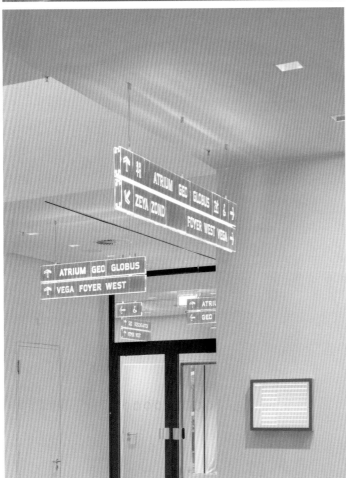

Dot
Shopping
Centre >>

Dot is a new technological Shopping in central Buenos Aires mostly targeted to women and young people and the logo comes from the architectural project.

Once the name and logo has been defined, Dot applied the Visual Identity to all items of communications as wayfinding, parking, publicity, printed material, etc. Dot colours – unique in Buenos Aires shoppings – express a friendly and dinamic palette dedicated to the mentioned target. The designers also design a type for the logo, later called Dot tipography.

Design Agency:
Shakespear SRL
Designer:
Juan Shakespear
Martina Mut
Gonzalo Strasser
Joaquin Viramonte
Client:
Dot Shopping Centre
Photography:
Alejandro Calderone
Location:
Argentina
Date:
2010

Galerias
Pacifico
Shopping
Centre >>

Galerias Pacifico is a down town shopping in Buenos Aires mostly dedicated to foreign visitors and high life. The logo has been applied to all items of communications as wayfinding, parking, publicity, printed material, etc.

Design Agency:
Shakespear SRL
Designer:
Juan Shakespear
Lorenzo Shakespear
Ronald Shakespear
Client:
Galerias Pacifico Shopping Centre
Photography:
Galerias Pacifico Shopping Centre
Location:
Argentina
Date:
2007

← **Planta baja**
Cajas

Atención Prefer
Empresas
Individuos

Gerencia

Stadium
Outlet >>

In the "in-store warehouse", classic warehouse design elements are used to create a contemporary look and feel. Stadium has since the end of 2009 opened eight outlets with huge success. The most profitable Stadium store is currently the #3 Stadium Outlet.

Design Agency:
BLINK
Client:
Stadium Outlet
Photography:
BLINK
Location:
Sweden
Date:
2010

40-70%

Sport har aldrig varit billigare!

Granngarden
Country Life
Stores >>

Simplistic, functional presentation with B2B-look and feel. The design is inspired by industrial farming with strong primary colours, wood, galvanised metal, logo burned onto material.

Design Agency:
BLINK
Client:
Granngarden Country Life Stores
Photography:
BLINK
Location:
Sweden
Date:
2010

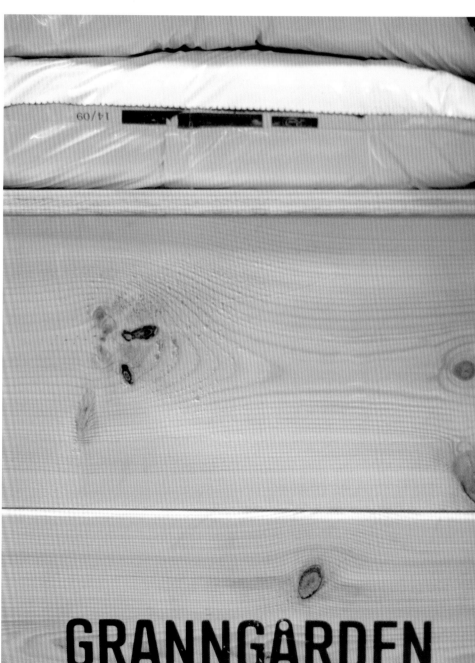

EN GRÄSMATTA ATT
VARA STOLT ÖVER

2 Klipp gräset ofta. Det gör gräsmattan tät och ogräset får svårt att trivas.

2 Lägg ut en markduk som släpper igenom luft och vatten – men inte ogräs.

3

Chinatown Mall >>

The Chinatown Mall in Fortitude Valley was first opened in 1987. In 2009, the Mall was redeveloped by a collaboration between architects from Brisbane's sister city, Shenzhen, Brisbane City Council and Urbis.
The new suite of signs reflects Chinese cultural elements whilst also referencing the new modern redevelopment.

Design Agency:
Dot Dash
Designer:
Irené Ostash
Client:
Brisbane City Council
Photography:
Irené Ostash
Location:
Australia
Date:
2010

Westfield
Shopping
Centre >>

Pearson Lloyd was commissioned to create a set of wayfinding products for the Westfield Shopping Centre in London. The object of the project was to create a comprehensive design language for the wayfinding products that could carry the different information and signage systems throughout the Shopping Centre. This included digital information points, digital advertising space, orientation signage and markers, as well as concierge desks, and information terminals.

Westfield is a large development with 1.5 million square metres of shopping space. A sleek and modern urban mall, the environment is to feel light and sophisticated, with lavish storefronts and spectacular features such as sweeping staircases and an undulating glass roof. The challenge lies in creating a set of wayfinding products that is at once expressive, yet complements the various features of this lush environment.

The result is a family of white, sculptural products that are at once impressive, yet unassuming. The forms are elegant and fluid to reflect Westfield's refined shopping experience. The forms morph organically to deliver the different wayfinding products. Made in Corian, these self-finished products can be easily maintained.

Design Agency:
Pearson Lloyd
Graphic Designer:
Atelier Works
Designer:
Pearson Lloyd
Photography:
Phil Sayer
Client:
Westfield London
Location:
London, UK
Date:
2008

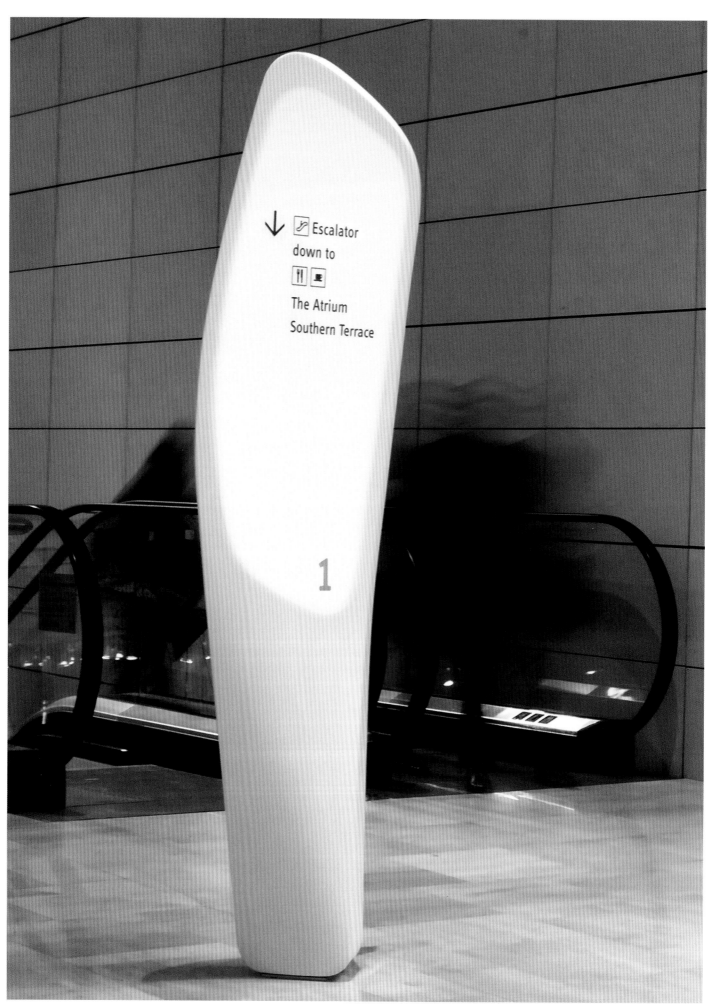

Maison
Corbeil
Furniture
Retailer >>

Maison Corbeil is a Montreal furniture retailer. Its products are characteristically simple, pure and elegant. Over the past thirty-five years, this local institution has become the first stop for the serious home decor shoppers. The company takes a global approach to home design, where established classics and the latest trends harmonise in a unique combination of perfect taste and comfort.

Maison Corbeil has entrusted Paprika studio with their brand development for many years. The designers aim for unfettered consistency that can evolve with the times. That means the design sticks to the company's precepts of simplicity and elegance for everything, be it a catalogue, prospectus, interior or exterior signage or their website.

Design Agency:
Paprika studio
Creative Director:
Louis Gagnon
Designer:
François Leclerc
David Guarnieri
Client:
Maison Corbeil
Location:
Japan
Date:
2010

Introduction

As principal of the environmental graphics consulting firm Formation, I know that there is a wealth of information readily available on the internet or in printed publication about wayfinding in healthcare. Much of the content describes how successful healthcare facilities realise that good wayfinding is synonymous with good patient flow, and that applying simple organisational, architectural and graphic principles not only reduces patient stress and anxiety, but can lead to improved patient outcomes, profitability, safety and staff utilisation. While all of this is true and important to us at Formation, I would like to focus on our approach.

Form Relationships with the Architect

Our office embraces a philosophy of working closely with the architect to integrate wayfinding into the architectural building design in order to optimise circulation through a facility and infuse a sense of intuitive guidance into the surroundings. This critical input provides architects with a patient-user viewpoint that addresses their emotional and physical needs, as well as assistance in solving the owner's demands for functional service spaces. Wayfinding systems can easily show benefits of reduced staff involvement with lost patients. Providing this level of new effectiveness in a new facility is in many ways the work of the environmental graphic designer – a specialist who represents the voice of the patient family.

Our best projects are the ones that we engage early in the design process and are completely in sync with the goals of the architect. We form a close working relationship with the architect and interior designer to understand or help create the design rationale of the overall project. This kinship and trust is important, because there are many projects in which we challenge the design of the building. We ask questions like "How can the physical space be altered to accomplish better circulation or clearer visual cues", "Can donor recognition be integrated into the architecture" to create visual landmarks, or "How does a patient know which door to enter, and can we identify the entrance in a more architectural way without a sign?" These are opportunities to simplify the visual clutter that typically comes with the additive nature of a "signage system".

Tell a Story

Conceiving an intuitive and expandable wayfinding strategy for a healthcare environment is a challenging engagement. Clients come to us to resolve issues that exceed simple signage solutions. Examples include naming and nomenclature inconsistencies that have existed for decades, integrating marketing messages and directions given via technology solutions, or creating comprehensive branded environments. Having a finger on the pulse of so many initiatives necessitates a well orchestrated story about the patient journey, illustrating the hospital's public image and the various interactions a visitor encounters.

By producing a detailed patient journey story, we describe the needs and conflicts of the patient, and give our work a sense of humanity. Stories typically begin from home with a pre-departure patient communications packet they receive with a customised map to their destination, brochures and a website for additional information. During their journey, the story describes how the address on their GPS technology is coordinated with the address of the hospital parking, how to get to the correct front door, and how they are greeted at the lobby. We direct them to the correct elevator, to the patient room, from patient room to an amenity (like the gift shop or cafeteria) and then back home. We paint the story with broad strokes about the overall experience, by always describing environmental conditions beyond the physical signage that effect the first time visitor's wayfinding experience. The story will inevitably tell the tale that less is more, and confirms that integration has tangible value in a complex environment.

Test the Design

Formation utilises qualitative and observational research to test several wayfinding system options with hospital user groups. The goal is to gain insight into how people will use the system, how they interact with spaces within the hospital, and what improvements or innovations are needed. This research allows us to uncover unspoken cultural and social patterns that shape visitor behaviours, and ultimately interpret this information to help form a wayfinding system recommendation for the hospital.

In order to ensure adequate collection of data from the diverse pool of visitors, we utilise focus group, quantitative survey and on-site interview based methodologies. In each method, wayfinding system options are presented to staff and visitor comprised focus groups. Each system showcases key features that distinguish it from the other option. We present large storyboards depicting a typical wayfinding scenario for each wayfinding option, followed by questionnaire surveys to gather initial user opinions. Subsequent focus group sessions are conducted to gather general comments from each group represented. On-site interviews are also conducted in a similar fashion with hospital visitors selected at random in the hospital waiting areas.

We can implement improvements to the wayfinding system based upon user input and identify different user needs (staff, outpatient visitors, inpatient visitors, patient guests, etc.). Additionally, we can implement the data retrieved to improve colour legibility, hospital nomenclature/naming conventions, fonts, character sizes and legibility. We gather information about which internal destinations should be highlighted on maps (key destinations) and the public path design as integrated into the wayfinding system. All of the findings and feedback gets shared with architect to influence any design tweaks.

Implement the Design

To ensure that our processes are implemented well, we typically get a reputable graphics fabricator involved early on in the project to assist us with construct-ability issues and to produce mock-ups for client comments. Architects and owners appreciate an advanced understanding of the quality and aesthetic of the signage because it eliminates the unknown at the very end of a project. This feedback allows for us to document the graphics with better accuracy and for pricing to meet the client's expectations.

In summary, Formation focuses on interactions with people, understanding the unique cultures of our clients and hopefully bringing humanity to our work. Our process allows us to create experiences that are considerate to the users, and integrated into the built environment.

Philip LeBlanc
Formation

The Zug Cantonal Hospital >>

The Zug Cantonal Hospital comprises three hospitals: the Department of Surgery, the Medical Clinic and the Women's Clinic. These priorities are complemented by the anesthesia/intensive care, diagnostic radiology and the emergency centre. Each year this hospital care for and treat approximately 8,700 inpatient and 30,000 outpatient patients.

Designalltag developed a comprehensive wayfinding strategy and master plan, then coordinated the three-year implementation of this strategy. Implementation activities included design development for all wayfinding components, construction documentation, and supervision of all fabrication and installation.

Design Agency:
Designalltag
Client:
Zuger Kantonsspital
Location:
Switzerland
Date:
2008 – 2010

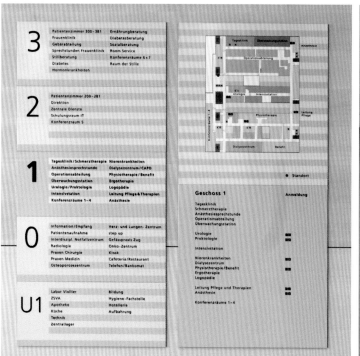

Koje 7

Koje 6

Koje 5
Koje 4
Koje 3

Nursing Home Pflegezen- trum Baar >>

The Care Centre Baar has been equipped with a modern architecture. The types of information have been incorporated into the colour and architecture. The project design parameters reflect the intent of the client, whose objective was to go beyond signs in developing a unique, site-specific wayfinding programme that works on a variety of levels to enhance the appearance, interest, and function of the hospital environment. Meetings with the client and architects explored opportunities to create a meaningful identity for the facility and different interior spaces. The designers created an appropriate, functional palette of options for the sign system programme.

Design Agency:
Designalltag
Client:
Pflegezentrum Baar
Location:
Switzerland
Date:
2008 – 2009

Lance
Armstrong
Cancer
Foundation
>>

Founded in 1997 by cancer survivor and champion cyclist Lance Armstrong, the Lance Armstrong Foundation (LAF) has raised more than $260 million for the fight against cancer.

fd2s designed a graphics programme that turns the building's public spaces into a venue for conveying the mission, history, and achievements of the LAF and its many constituent groups, while also providing opportunities to recognise LAF donors. A recurring motif of the programme is a yellow band with recessed or cut-out type, which is a tribute the foundation's most recognised symbol, the yellow wristbands that have raised tens of millions of dollars, one dollar at a time.

A low-key, backlit, stainless-steel panel on a repurposed warehouse wall serves as the building's primary identification element, and the large yellow band in the glass-walled reception area can also be seen from outside. The yellow band in the lobby makes a strong statement, replicating the organisation's signature "Livestrong" wristbands.

Design Agency:
fd2s
Photography:
David Omer
Client:
Lance Armstrong Foundation
Location:
USA
Date:
2009

ATTITUDE IS EVERYTHING.

The University of Texas M. D. Anderson Cancer Centre >>

One of the world's largest and most prestigious healthcare institutions, M. D. Anderson Cancer Centre operates in an enormous – and growing – physical environment. fd2s began the project with an in-depth analysis of the needs of M. D. Anderson patients and visitors, and the staff that serves them. The elements concepted, designed, documented, and produced by fd2s in the implementation of this strategy were extensive, and the effort involved close coordination with staff from throughout M. D. Anderson, ranging from facilities and information technology to marketing and public relations.

The wayfinding system is based on a "pathway and landmark" approach, which helps to simplify the extremely complex environment. The signage components' modular frame system uses digital output produced on-site that can be replaced without disturbing walls and interior finishes. Access is icon-based, and the entire system is designed to accommodate users with varying language skills and cognitive abilities.

Design Agency:
fd2s
Photography:
David Omer
Client:
The University of Texas M. D. Anderson Cancer Centre
Location:
USA
Date:
2008

4 **Outpatient MF**

2

The Tree S

access Skybridge

Rotary Ho

Administrative

Appearances

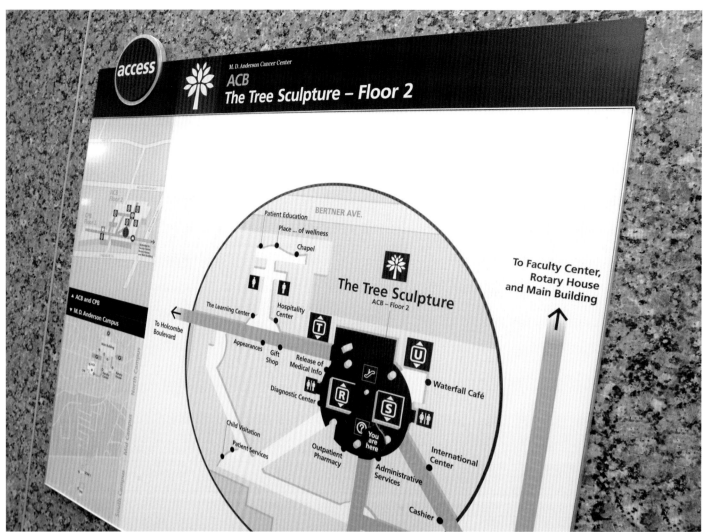

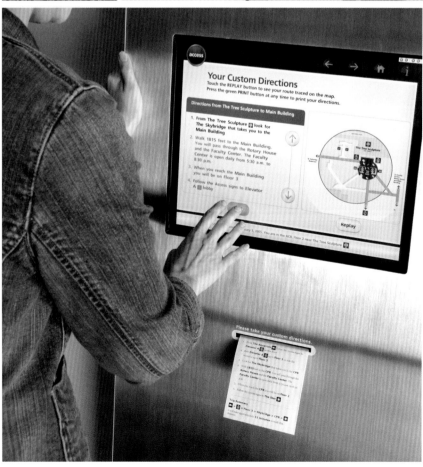

real people

"I earn it."

Warren Meredith. | Spinal Cord Tumor

real hope

Warren's Story

Parents like to believe that kids "bounce back" after illness or injury. Well, Warren Meredith certainly did. The day he turned two years old, doctors found a tumor on his spinal cord. Warren survived, and despite a year of chemotherapy and six weeks of radiation, "all he remembers are happy thoughts about playing with his nurses and friends," Warren's mother, Holly, says. He's got more important things to worry about now, like earning "brag vest" patches in Cub Scouts Pack 239. As for Holly, enough cancer-free birthdays have now passed that she's beginning to bounce back too. "Slowly, I'm letting go of the rough times," she confides.

Children's
Hospital
Boston >>

Children's Hospital Boston asked Two Twelve to create a new campus wayfinding and signage master plan for its 130-year old, 5-building campus. The plan included analysis and strategy for wayfinding and signage, the design of sign types and graphic standards, and oversight of the initial pilot implementation in selected areas of the hospital.

Design Agency:
Two Twelve
Creative Director:
David Gibson
Cesar Sanchez
Designer:
Ellen Conant
Chris Dina
Sun Yang
Dominic Borgia
Photography:
Anton Grassl
Client:
Children's Hospital Boston
Location:
USA
Date:
2004

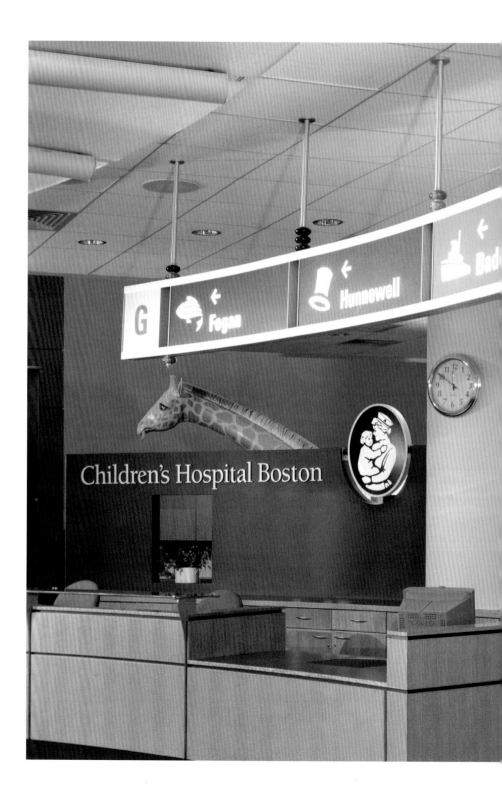

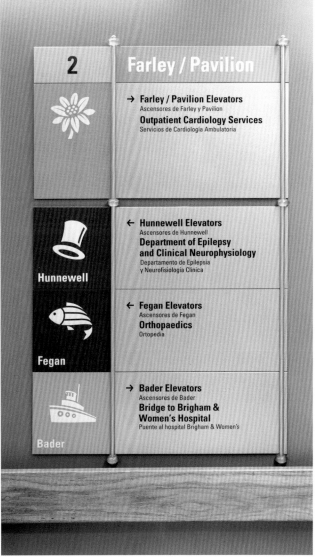

CHOC
Children's
Hospital >>

Formation is providing wayfinding strategy and design services including interior, exterior and donor recognition campaigns for the new 39,532-square-metre hospital tower. Formation was initially involved in the building and campus design, allowing Formation the opportunity to fully integrate identification, wayfinding and donor graphics into the architecture. Floor patterns, sculptural details, oversized dimensional copy and kinetic sculpture help engage children while aiding in wayfinding and the overall visitor experience. Wayfinding was a major element, with travel and navigation guides woven seamlessly into the interiors.

Design Agency:
Formation
Creative Director:
David Hoffer, Philip LeBlanc
Designer:
David Hoffer
Philip LeBlanc
Erich Theaman
Photography:
Philip LeBlanc
Client:
FKP Architects
Location:
USA
Date:
2006 – 2012

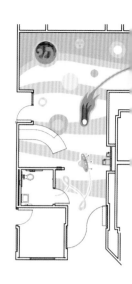

2 Pla
Scal

14' 6"

1 Pri
Scal

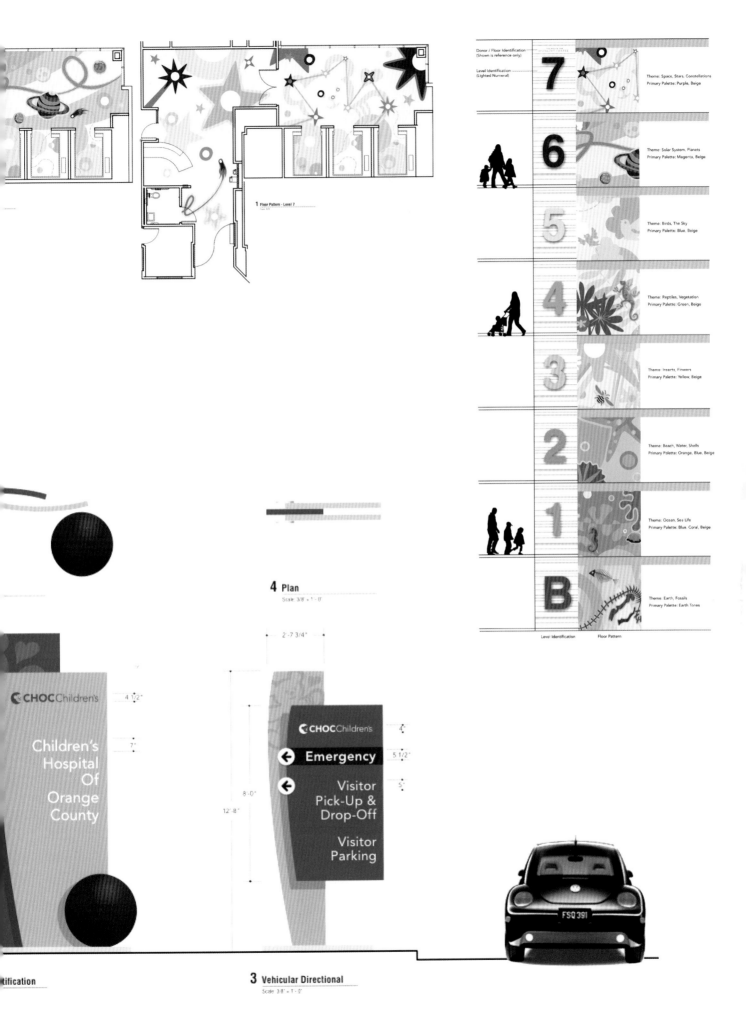

1 Floor Pattern - Level 7
Scale N/A

Donor / Floor Identification
(Shown is reference only)

Level Identification
(Lighted Numeral)

7 Theme: Space, Stars, Constellations
Primary Palette: Purple, Beige

6 Theme: Solar System, Planets
Primary Palette: Magenta, Beige

5 Theme: Birds, The Sky
Primary Palette: Blue, Beige

4 Theme: Reptiles, Vegetation
Primary Palette: Green, Beige

3 Theme: Insects, Flowers
Primary Palette: Yellow, Beige

2 Theme: Beach, Water, Shells
Primary Palette: Orange, Blue, Beige

1 Theme: Ocean, Sea Life
Primary Palette: Blue, Coral, Beige

B Theme: Earth, Fossils
Primary Palette: Earth Tones

Level Identification   Floor Pattern

4 Plan
Scale: 3/8" = 1' - 0'

2'-7 3/4"

CHOC Children's

4 1/2"

Children's
Hospital
Of
Orange
County

7"

8'-0"

12'-8"

CHOC Children's   4"

← **Emergency**   5 1/2"

← Visitor
Pick-Up &
Drop-Off   5"

Visitor
Parking

FSQ 391

tification

3 Vehicular Directional
Scale: 3/8" = 1' - 0'

Life
Science
Plaza >>

Formation provided logo design, place making and wayfinding design services for the exterior, interior and parking garage of this 27,871-square-metre 13-storey medical office building/hospital located in the Texas Medical Centre. The building tenants include medical offices as well as a 68-bed long-term acute care hospital. There is a health club facility that anchors the east end of the project and a public park at the west side of the project. The building acheived LEED gold certification.

Design Agency:
Formation
Creative Director:
David Hoffer
Philip LeBlanc
Designer:
David Hoffer
Philip LeBlanc
Erich Theaman
Photography:
Chan Do
Client:
Jones Lang LaSalle
Location:
USA
Date:
2007

caution:
pedestrian
crossing

level 2

life Science plaza

JONES LANG
LASALLE   1300

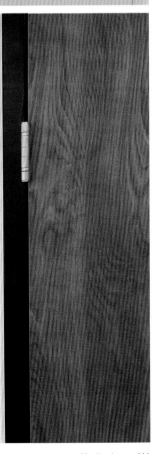

Nationwide Children's Hospital >>

Nationwide Children's Hospital is ranked as one of the nation's ten largest children's hospitals and pediatric research centres. To begin the engagement, Formation completed a comprehensive wayfinding experience audit and onsite focus group research to understand the complexities of the campus and behaviours of the various users. Data from this research is being used to inform a unique and personalised wayfinding experience for Nationwide Children's Hospital. An important component of this experience was reevaluating the way hospital staff described destinations when giving directions. Formation found that in many cases, the staff used conflicting names for many of the primary destinations, causing confusion for visitors. Formation is currently implementing a new nomenclature and naming convention for all hospital destinations.

In addition to the New Hospital Tower, Formation has been engaged to implement the interior and exterior wayfinding master plan for the 138,844-square-metre renovation of the existing inpatient facilities, outpatient facilities, support and office facilities, and parking structures. Working with the hospital Foundation, Formation is providing standards for a comprehensive donor recognition system as well as specialty donor campaigns. When completed, Nationwide Children's Hospital is expected to be the second largest pediatric hospital and research centre in America.

Design Agency:
Formation
Ralph Appelbaum Associates
Creative Director:
David Hoffer
Philip LeBlanc
Designer:
David Hoffer
Philip LeBlanc
Erich Theaman
Photography:
Philip LeBlanc
Client:
Nationwide Children's Hospital
Location:
USA
Date:
2007-2018 Phased Implementation

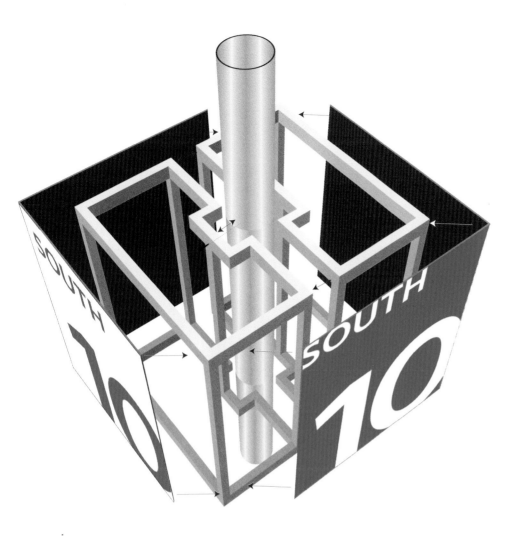

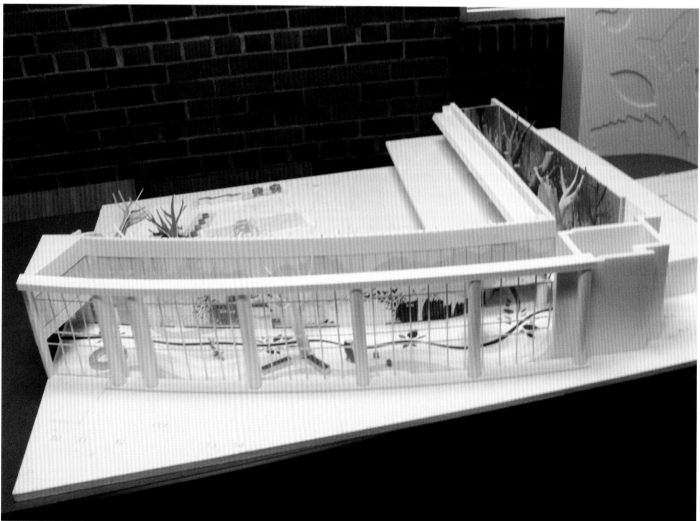

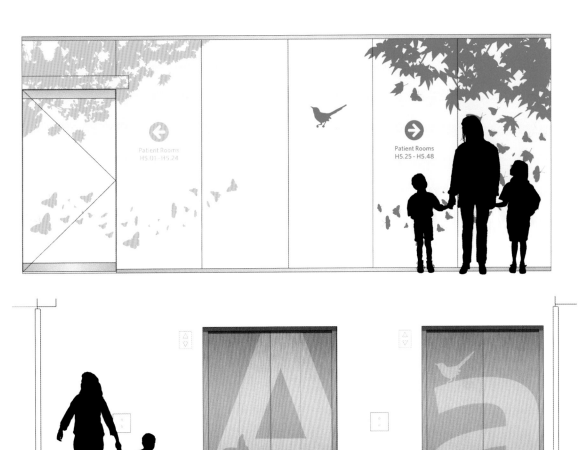

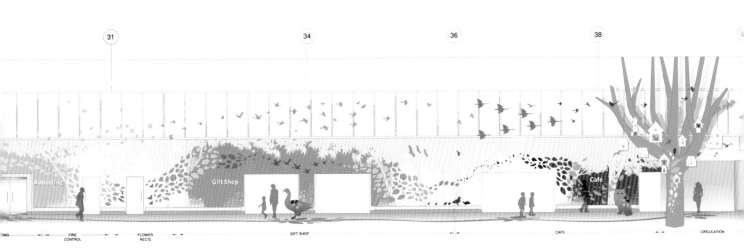

Auburn Hospital >>

Auburn Hospital is a 120-bed acute care health facility on the eastern border of Sydney The West Area Health Service. Buro North was enlisted to create signage design for this complex, busy and stressful hospital environment. A strict colour palette was chosen to work with all the interiors and with the overall hospital theming while maintaining a high level of legibility and wayfinding function. Pattern was employed as a visual language to strengthen and coordinate with the hospital's overall theme and art/feature wall.

Design Agency:
Buro North
Designer:
Soren Luckins
Dave Williamson
Tom Allnut
Photography:
Brett Boardman
Client:
Brookfield Multiplex
Location:
Australia
Date:
2009

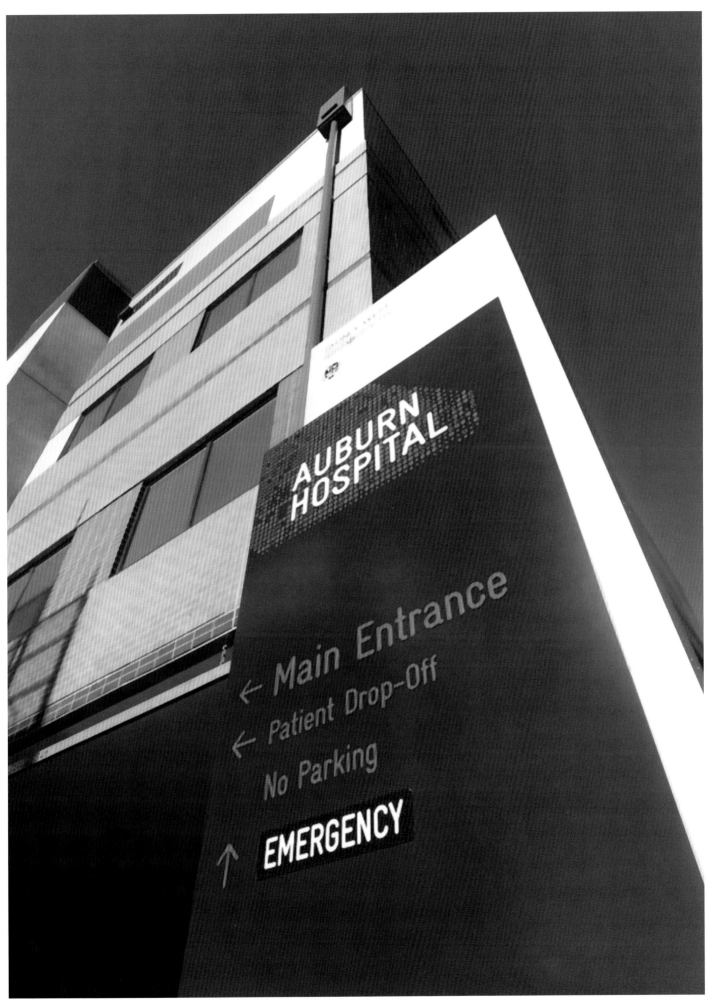

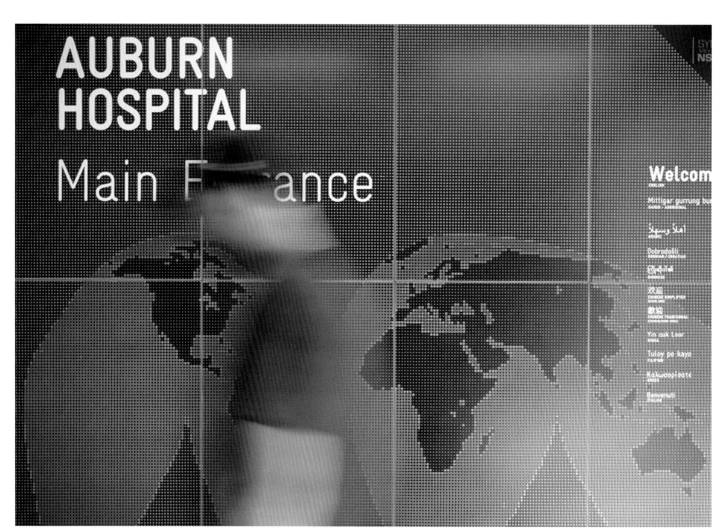

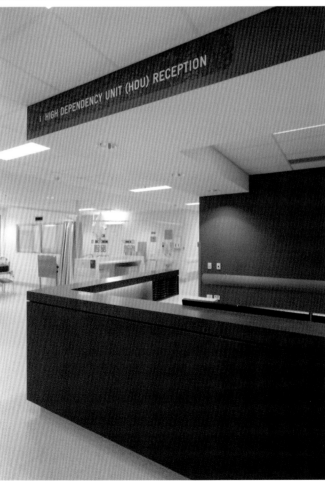

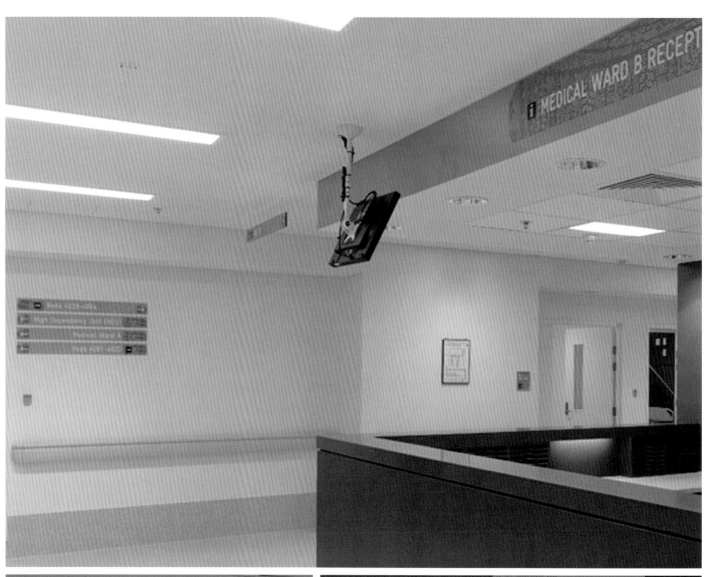

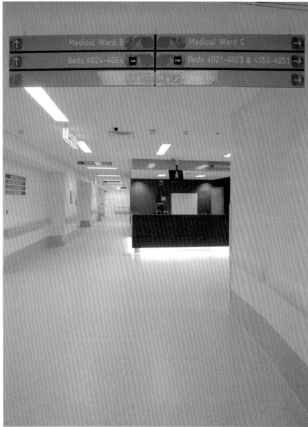

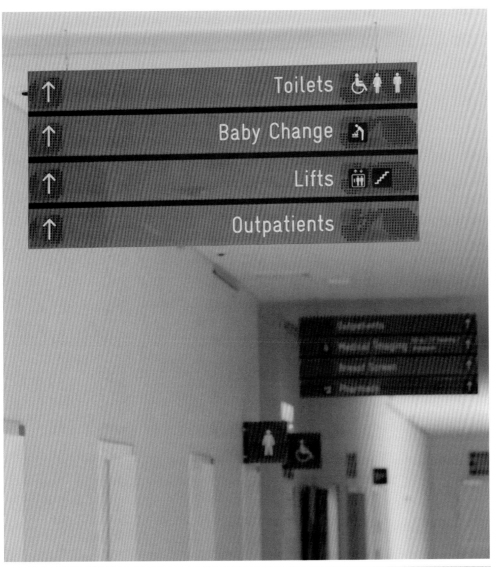

The Texas
Medical
Centre >>

In developing the wayfinding master plan, fd2s worked very closely with TMC staff, as well as with members of the TMC Ad Hoc Committee on Wayfinding. Members of this committee were briefed regularly on the status of the project, and also participated in a number of work sessions. In addition, fd2s team members also met directly with high-level representatives of TMC member institutions, gathering information about the institutions' immediate needs and future expansion projects, and generally working to build a consensus for the concepts being developed, which helped to smooth the later efforts to achieve buy-in from all stakeholders.

The underlying logic of the wayfinding system ties particular destinations to landmarks, which take the form of large "numbered entrance" monuments. Directional elements on roadways leading to the Medical Centre guide users to these landmarks, and from there more specific wayfinding signage takes them to the appropriate institution entrance.

Design Agency:
fd2s
Creative Director:
Mark Denton
Designer:
Mark Denton
Photography:
David Omer
Client:
The Texas Medical Centre
Location:
USA
Date:
2007

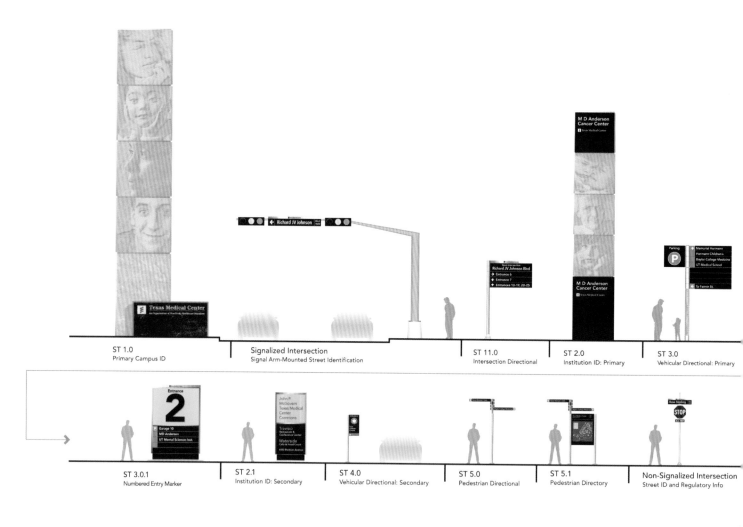

ST 1.0
Primary Campus ID

Signalized Intersection
Signal Arm-Mounted Street Identification

ST 11.0
Intersection Directional

ST 2.0
Institution ID: Primary

ST 3.0
Vehicular Directional: Primary

ST 3.0.1
Numbered Entry Marker

ST 2.1
Institution ID: Secondary

ST 4.0
Vehicular Directional: Secondary

ST 5.0
Pedestrian Directional

ST 5.1
Pedestrian Directory

Non-Signalized Intersection
Street ID and Regulatory Info

Marin Health
& Wellness
Campus >>

Square Peg Design developed the wayfinding strategy and signing programme for an innovative new health and wellness campus comprising of six buildings all built to LEED-NC Gold standard. Square Peg worked with the architect and client to design a graphics solution which establishes and integrates the property's identity throughout the interior and exterior signing and campus wayfinding system.

Design Agency:
Square Peg Design
Creative Derector:
Scott Cuyler
Designer:
Susan Bowers
Katie Miller
Photography:
Susan Bowers
RMW Architecture & Interiors
Client:
Marin County
Location:
USA
Date:
2008

Transportation Wayfinding

1. "The best way to predict the future is to design it."
   Buckminster Fuller

These large scale works are highly complex by their very nature, because of the huge number of requirements involved, by their multidisciplinary nature, and because of the changing socioeconomic conditions in which they take place. From the standpoint of design, these are paradigmatic projects and the international experience often confirms that they have played an epic role in the history of design. This permanent call that takes design to the public landscape and makes it land on the concrete of cities and live and activate the lives of cities and people, gives sense to our work and naturally becomes a way of looking at our profession.

Finally, if design is not good for making people live better, it's not good at all.

The fundamental factor in this breed of projects is order.

One major requirement for this kind of Systems is a very clear visual structure that enables users to access information instantly and accurately. Predictability is of the essence in order to facilitate a rapid learning of the semiotic network, where users establish a pragmatic dialogue with the signs and choose their options. Predictability is crucial in terms of location, size, colours, verbal and pictographic messages.

With the passage of time, our avid information-seeking society has become increasingly complex and has created the need for more and improved vehicles of information, with a view to a better understanding.

This process has never been smooth. On the contrary, the amount of unnecessary information is always larger than the amount of relevant information. Our visual environment is a reflection of that complexity.

2. "If you don't know where you are going, any road will take you there."
   Lewis Carroll

A transportation wayfinding system calls for a profound specific study that considers the context in which signs are to be used. Architectural constraints, lighting conditions, the complexities of circulation, adequate locations of the signs, and the quality of the messages addressed to wide audiences.

Graphic, typographic, chromatic, technologic and location subsystems, these five subsystems, acting jointly and separately, determine the efficiency of a wayfinding system.

The graphic subsystem tends to establish the visual power of the tools used; the typographic subsystem determines the legibility of messages; the chromatic subsystem determines the ability to codify in a pragmatic fashion; the technologic subsystem determines the strength and quality of the signs. Finally, the location subsystem defines the most effective location of the signs in terms of perception and self-protection to avoid defacement or destruction of the signs.

Wayfinding is understood today as a vital need in any transportation system, in terms of ordering the flow of users, but it is also a significant element in a plan that seeks to renovate the "landscape". Historically, this landscape has tended to become polluted by a number of unplanned elements. In a comprehensive project, where advertising and stores have a strong presence, signs are the voice of the place and a part of its identity.

3. "In theory, theory is exactly the same as practice. In practice it's not."
   Rob Roach

The strong conditioning elements in the urban landscape, and especially the widespread presence of advertising and the proliferation of stores, force designers to make certain decisions to provide pragmatic communications with the necessary strength and identity. In this context, this can only be achieved through scale, repetition and adequate location. The idea is to generate a communication channel that sets the voice and tone of the issuer from a constant – and accordingly predictable – location, with a view to prioritising information and the connection with the public.

4. "It isn't that they can't see the solution. It's that they can't see the problem."
   G. K. Chesterton

Any transportation system is formed by two basic dimensions. Firstly there is infrastructure and all the elements involved in it, the comprehensive service network. Secondly, there is communication, which, through a number of functional elements, enables users to understand and use the service. We call this second dimension the "semiotic network". Pragmatic communication happens by means of an efficient wayfinding system. Ever since the creation of railways, airports, bus stations, amusement parks as means of mass transportation, maps have been a concern and a challenge for engineers, managers and professional designers.

Illustrious precedents such as the pioneer London Underground map (by Henry C. Beck), or the New York Subway map (by Massimo Vignelli) have turned this particular piece of work into a design classic, a prototypical expression of the social function of design and a paradigm in terms of mass design and rationalist treatment of information.

This graphic configuration expresses the "menu" of navigation, destinations and exchanges to the public with some substantial benefits in terms of perception. It establishes a way of "reading" the place. Sensible and intuitive signage systems are created by designers who understand the complexities of public spaces, the particular environment of the project in question, and the expected performance and functions of the signs. Designers of signage systems decipher the audience's codes. Signs are active expressions of identity that go beyond just giving directions and solving basic circulation and communication problems. They are instruments that help build a house style, a tone of voice, a dialogue with the audience.

They are part of the citizen's daily life. Signs not only are there; they must act as if they have always been there. They must become visible when the decision of a destination has to be made, do their job, and then become part of the surroundings again. Jock Kinneir had a deep significance for us back in the 1970s. The epic narrative of his programme for the UK highwaysturned him into a reference.

The way he managed his relationship with the traffic engineers, architects, and urban planners was as significant as the pragmatic representation of the "Road Ahead as a Vector Sign", from a historical point of view, perhaps his most remarkable contribution at the time. "Man speaks in small letters. He shouts in capital letters," Jock Kinneir used to say. It has been said that humankind has the public signs it deserves, although it is almost sure that the Roman Empire did not deserve something as beautiful as the Trajan's typographic frontispieces. Facing such an assignment, adds Jock Kinneir, is a moment of truth for a designer, because it challenges his/her skills, integrity, and power of permanence.

Ronald Shakespear
Buenos Aires, September 29 2010

Buenos Aires Underground Subte >>

Buenos Aires is a city with a rich cultural and urban heritage. The recovery of access gate as an institutional flag was regarded as a natural extension of the visual grammar inside the network, yet with a technological proposal that emphasises the notion of modernity, strength, urban scale and character of the issuer. Providing an underground transportation service and the connection between the worlds "above" and "below" has a deep emblematic significance. With the new logo the "lines" concept was enphasised by using historic colours to identify them. The latest contribution in this area has been the new meaning given to the Subway as an urban brand.

The designers have also discovered that people use expressions such as "I take the green one" or "I take the red one". This clearly shows the value attributed to their preferred usual subway lines. From a conceptual perspective, the new visual expression of the "Subte" brand has been generated through an emphasis on the popular term, reinforcing it and emphasising the notion of LINE in the logo, so that the colour that identifies each line would be more clearly expressed at the entrance of every station.

Design Agency:
Shakespear SRL
Designer:
Juan Shakespear
Lorenzo Shakespear
Ronald Shakespear
Client:
Subte
Location:
Argentina
Date:
2008

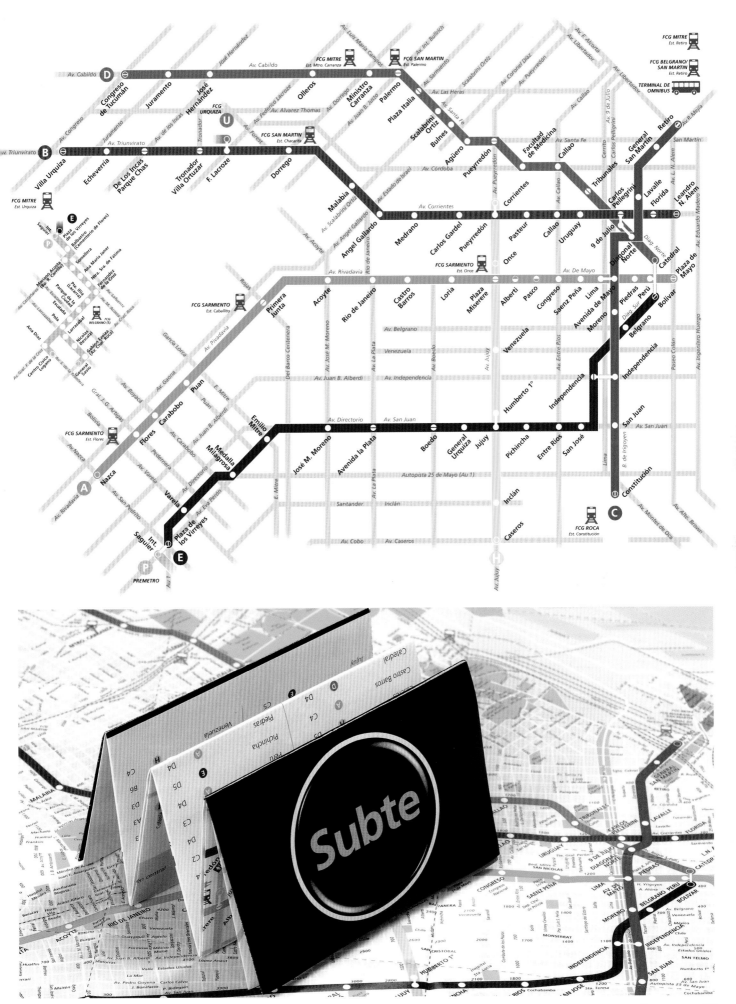

Tren de la
Costa >>

The sun comes from the east,from the river, and so does the train. This was the source for the design of the brand, and all its implementations have been technologically treated to reflect that adequately.

The project team carefully studied the "mother" chromatic source of the project from several perspectives. Ral 6005 green was the choice – a paradigmatic one – for the wayfinding signs and the train's graphic skin. That was the starting point of the chromatic features of all communication elements in the project. The red nerve that goes through the green, like a living path, on the trains themselves and on every sign, seeks not only to connect the project to the iconography of railway restoration – the railways of childhood and nostalgia – but also to emphasise the ecologic factor that was the project's premise.

Design Agency:
Shakespear SRL
Designer:
Juan Shakespear
Lorenzo Shakespear
Ronald Shakespear
Photography:
Juan Hitters
Client:
Tren de la Costa
Location:
Argentina
Date:
2008

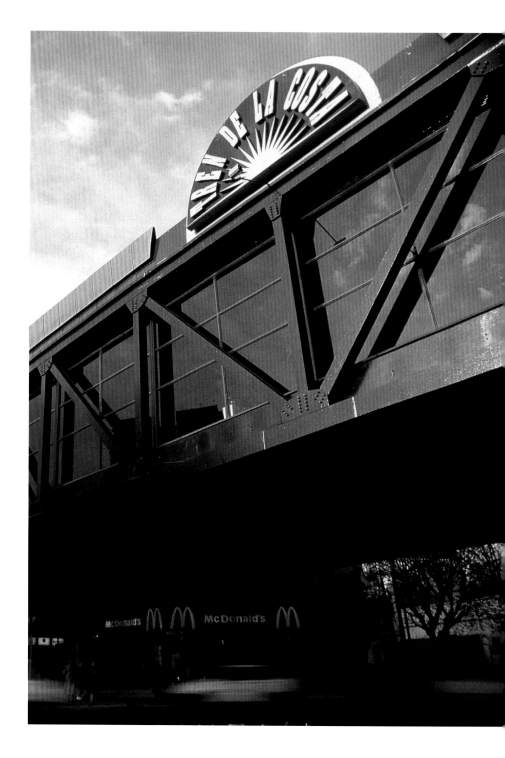

Amtrak
Acela
Stations >>

C&VE's Acela signage programme created a strong brand identity for Amtrak's high-speed rail service. The programme was imposed on the entire passenger experience, and was designed for a diverse range of stations along Amtrak's northeast travel corridor. It incorporated variable message displays for changeable information. The programme was developed to promote signage uniformity from station to station with minimum custom fitting. The sensuously curved "airfoil" shape became the stylistic nucleus of the signage programme. Gate identification signs use flashing gate and track numbers to indicate arriving trains. Hinged sign housings protect the internal systems from the elements and provide easy access for maintenance.

Design Agency:
Calori & Vanden-Eynden / Design Consultants
Art Director:
David Vanden-Eynden
Chris Calori
Designer:
David Vanden-Eynden
Chris Calori
Jordan Marcus
Denise Funaro
Photography:
Elliott Kaufman
Client:
National Railroad Passenger Corporation
Location:
USA
Date:
Ongoing

Port
Imperial
Ferry
Terminal >>

Calori & Vanden-Eynden's goals for the Weehawken Ferry Terminal were to enhance passenger orientation, identify facilities, complement the terminal's architectural detailing, and reinforce the brand image of the ferry service provider, New York Waterways (NYW).

The terminal's clean, contemporary architecture alludes to a ship in its exterior elevations. Accordingly, the signage hardware system is expressed as a series of sleek, white "boat" shapes attached to ceilings and walls with inverted conical aluminium pylons based on the building's column shapes. The sign graphics are bright and highly legible, reinforcing NYW's identity by utilising the company's red, white, and blue colours and typeface.

Design Agency:
Calori & Vanden-Eynden / Design Consultants
Art Director:
Chris Calori
Designer:
Chris Calori
David Vanden-Eynden
Denise Funaro
Photography:
Mark Reinertson
Client:
New York Waterways
New Jersey Transit
Location:
USA
Date:
2006

St.Gallen
Brühltor –
Passage >>

The Brühltor was once a city gate. It connects the old town with the Museum Quarter. It is the western access to the expanded and redesigned City Parking Brühltor in 2006. It had been planned since 1999. The orientation problem for visitors, who are not familiar within the area, remained despite the creative measures: it is underground and man has no relation with the outside world. There is no daylight, so it's impossible to find the direction. In addition, the underpass has four entrances and exits with two lifts and escalators. The Inform GmbH is a specialist planner for signage and designer for visual communication. Signage provides people spatial orientation in complex spaces and situations. The designers want the greatest contrast for good legibility in light environmental situations; the arrows should be given one colour. It would have been required in red from CI , but red signs are not ideal for the visually impaired. So they have chosen green arrows.

Design Agency:
Inform GmbH
Designer:
Felix Hartmann
Marc Frick
Tristan Hartmann
Client:
Hochbauamt St.Gallen
Location:
Switzerland
Date:
2008

Willawong
Bus
Depot >>

The 6-hectare Willawong Bus Depot is Brisbane City Council's largest bus storage facility. The facility includes a state-of-the-art depot administration building, staff recreational facilities, garage and workshops, refuelling and detailing building and associated car parking and hardstand for over 200 buses.

The bold industrial aesthetic of the sign programme helps form the character of the site. Sign hardware and graphics draw upon elements from within the main roads traffic sign system, components in which the bus driver interacts with on a daily basis.

The wayfinding system included external and interior signage as well as surface graphic treatments to bus hardstand and safeway zones. The strategy focuses on providing clear delineation between visitor and staff areas.

Design Agency:
Dot Dash
Designer:
Heath Pedrola
Photography:
Heath Pedrola
Client:
Brisbane City Council
Location:
Australia
Date:
2009

FIRE SAFETY DOOR
DO NOT OBSTRUCT

Tyre Fitting Bay

BikeWay
in Lisbon >>

This lane runs along the river Tagus, in Lisbon, and with its 7,362 metres it crosses different urban spaces, each one demanding different solutions. The goal was to define a new urban environment beyond the bikeway, in order to improve this area along the river. The selection of compatible and existing materials was considered in order to make clear the readability and use of the new system. The coating materials added are used to strengthen the material unity that characterises the space, creating a smooth and adherent surface resembling the Portuguese basalt pavements. All the signs, symbols and words, establish boundaries, guidance and info are in white paint. The plan tells us a story, takes us, guides us and seduces us along this route. As we pass by, points of interest are revealed, touristic, cultural and natural ones, as some useful signage for transports, stops or break points. Over estabilised pavements, graphic "incisions" were made, in order to preserve the existing surface, consisting of circles and polygons made of metal, filled with asphalt, making an everlasting system of signs. It's in the use of Alberto Caeiro's poem about this river, or in the onomatopoeic intervention illustrating the sounds of the bridge, that the basic needs of communication are exceeded.

Design Agency:
P-06 Atelier
GLOBAL landscape architecture
Art Director:
Nuno Gusmão,
João Gomes da Silva
Creative Director:
Nuno Gusmão
Estela Pinto
Pedro Anjos
Designer:
Giuseppe Greco
Miguel Matos
Photography:
João Silveira Ramos
Giuseppe Greco
Client:
(APL) Lisbon Seaport
(EDP) Energias de Portugal
(CML) Lisbon City Hall
Location:
Portugal
Date:
2009

QUELES QUE A ENCONTRAM.   NINGUÉM NUNCA PENSOU NO QUE HÁ PARA ALÉM   DO RIO DA MINHA ALDE

PELO TEJO VAI-SE PARA
O MUNDO.
PARA ALÉM DO TEJO HÁ
A AMÉRICA
E A FORTUNA DAQUELES
QUE A ENCONTRAM.
NINGUÉM NUNCA PENSOU
NO QUE HÁ PARA ALÉM
DO RIO DA MINHA ALDEIA.

John F. Kennedy International Airport >>

GNU Group developed a wayfinding master plan and implementation plan for this multi-phased construction of American Airlines' hub to the EU and Central Asia. This 38-gate, 148,645-square-metre terminal includes a 3,500-passenger-per-hour Customs & Border Protection facility, and over 2,500 signs.

Design Agency:
GNU Group
Creative Director:
Tom Donnelly
Designer:
Darcy Belgarde
Photography:
Tom Donnelly
Client:
American Airlines
DMJM Aviation
TranSystems
Location:
USA
Date:
2008

San Bernardino International Airport >>

GNU Group was responsible for the design and management of a comprehensive branding and wayfinding sign programme for this conversion of the former Norton Air Force Base into a commercial airport. The project scope included roadway, parking and terminal signs, and graphic image walls, depicting points of interest in the greater Los Angeles area, at the security checkpoint.

Design Agency:
GNU Group
Creative Director:
Tom Donnelly
Designer:
Tom Donnelly
Chris Uy
Photography:
Tom Donnelly
Client:
Norton Development, LLC
TranSystems
Location:
USA
Date:
2010

Connect
Sheffield
Pedestrian
System >>

Connect Sheffield is the first fully integrated DDA compliant pedestrian system in the UK. The project is unique in its ambition to develop a single information culture throughout the city which combines both pedestrian and transport information in a fully co-ordinated manner. Connect Sheffield is comprised of an extensive system of on-street information delivery including pedestrian map panels, bus stop flags and tram stop displays. Underpinning the range of information design elements is a robust hierarchy and methodology for information planning that delivers appropriate information with consistency and continuity for all users including residents, visitors and the business community. The primary physical feature of the product is a chamfered stainless steel edge frame that allows the graphic content of each unit to bleed fully to all edges. It also acts to protect the backlit low ion glass information panels from physical damage and reduces the sense of volume of the product on the street.

Design Agency:
PearsonLloyd
Photography:
PearsonLloyd
Client:
City of Sheffield
Location:
UK
Date:
2007

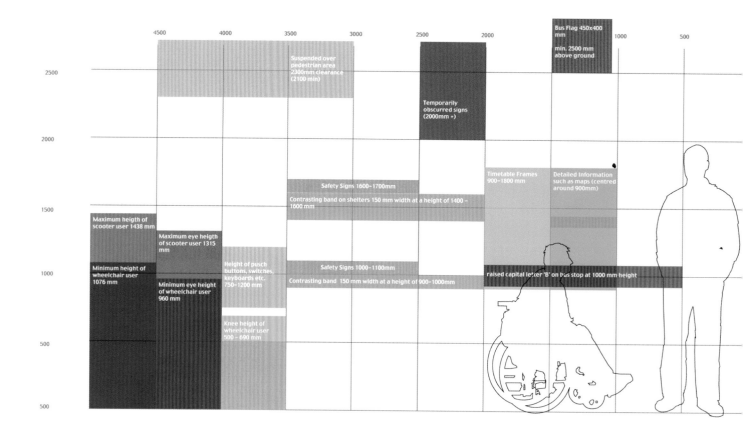

Maximum heigth of scooter user 1438 mm

Maximum eye heigth of scooter user 1315 mm

Minimum height of wheelchair user 1076 mm

Minimum eye height of wheelchair user 960 mm

Height of pusch buttons, switches, keyboards etc. 750~1200 mm

Knee height of wheelchair user 500 ~ 690 mm

Suspended over pedestrian area 2300mm clearance (2100 min)

Temporarily obscurred signs (2000mm +)

Bus Flag 450x400 mm

min. 2500 mm above ground

Safety Signs 1600~1700mm

Contrasting band on shelters 150 mm width at a height of 1400 – 1600 mm

Safety Signs 1000~1100mm

Contrasting band 150 mm width at a height of 900~1000mm

Timetable Frames 900~1800 mm

Detailed Information such as maps (centred around 900mm)

raised capital letter 'B' on bus stop at 1000 mm height

Welcome to Sheffield Station

Transport services

Facilities within the Station

Glossop Road
West End

Glossop Road
West End

Welcome to
Arundel Gate Interchange
City & regional bus services

Bus Stop
MF3 Moorfoot
The Moor

3   4   22
97 97A M29

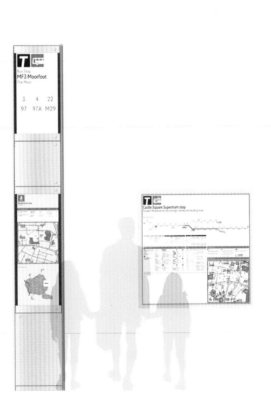

Van Nuys
Flyaway >>

The Van Nuys Flyaway is part of the Los Angeles World Airports' system of regional satellite depots that service Los Angeles Airport (LAX) via a park-and-ride bus system. As part of the recent renovation and expansion of the facility, Sussman/Prejza designed a new identity/logo for the Flyaway, which in turn became the starting point for work on the bus graphics and the facility's wayfinding. The Flyaway facility in Van Nuys is designed to look and feel like an extension of a modern airport, an objective shared by the graphics programme. The transit buses, which are the heart of the system, are beautiful and more importantly visible at busy LAX and on the freeways.

Design Agency:
Sussman/Prejza & Co., Inc.
Creative Director:
Paul Prejza
Miles Mazzie
Designer:
Hillary Jaye
Hsin-Hsien Tsai
Photography:
Jim Simmons
Client:
Los Angeles World Airport
Location:
USA
Date:
2006

Terminal
Entrance

Ticket
Purchase

Bus Departure

Tickets

VAN NUYS → LAX

City of Mound/Mound Harbour District >>

The sign and wayfinding system consists of over thirty-two unique signtypes from area identification to directional maps, and finally, standard regulatory signage. The sign design compliments the area history as reflected in surrounding bridge design and the street landscape.

The wayfinding signage will target commuters by promoting the commuting options offered by the park and ride and bike trails.

Signage integrates the concept of "Interconnectedness" into the visitor and user experience. The interconnectedness of the Mound Harbour District site is pertinent to surrounding areas and the transit links via water/land as a hub linking boats, trains, auto, bicycles, pedestrians, bus and auto traffic.

The design creates and communicates the excitement, size, and scope of the Mound Harbour District as a vibrant city centre "Main Street" with amenities including: Lost Lake Canal, bike paths, roadways, and future LRT linking neighbouring communities of Minnetrista, St. Boni, Spring Park, Wayzata, and Navarre.

Design Agency:
Visual Communications, Inc.
Creative Director:
Richard Lang
Graphic designer:
Jesse Yungner
Designer:
Constance Carlson
Graphic Designer:
Jesse Yungner
Photography:
Richard Lang
Client:
City of Mound
Location:
USA
Date:
2009

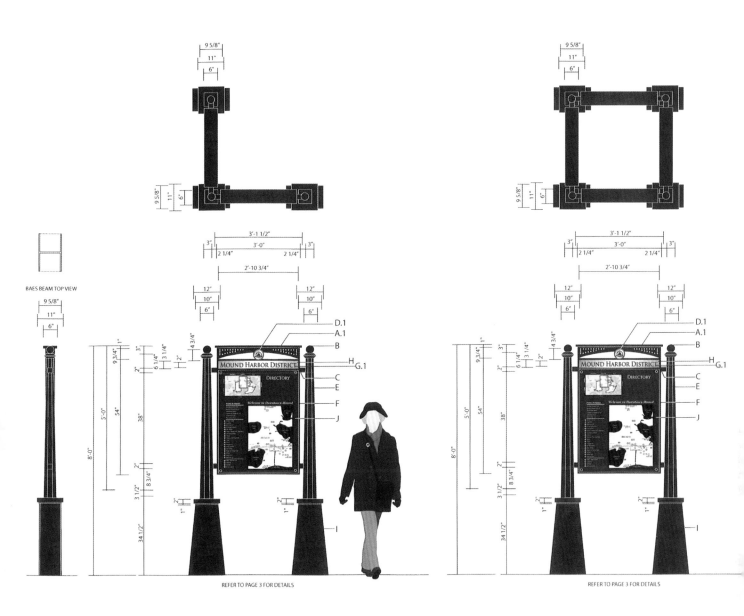

REFER TO PAGE 3 FOR DETAILS

REFER TO PAGE 3 FOR DETAILS

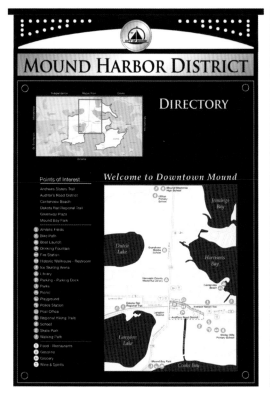

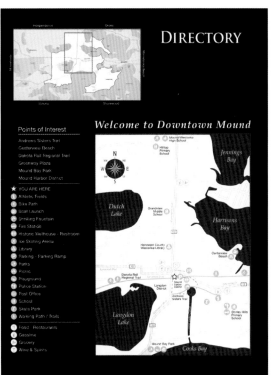

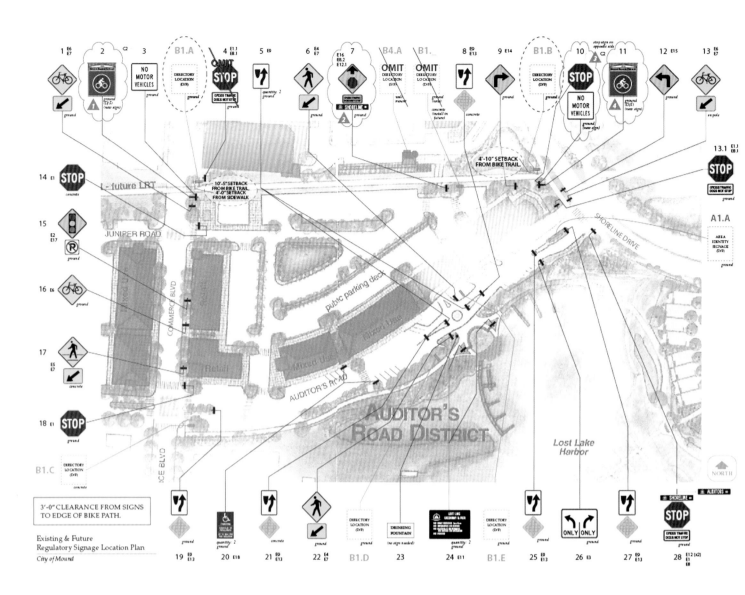

14 E1 STOP concrete

15 E2 E17 ℗ ground

16 E6 🚲 ground

17 E5 E7 ground

18 E1 STOP ground

B1.C DIRECTORY LOCATION (DVR) concrete

3'-0" CLEARANCE FROM SIGNS TO EDGE OF BIKE PATH.

Existing & Future
Regulatory Signage Location Plan
City of Mound

1 E6 E7 · 2 Q2 · 3 NO MOTOR VEHICLES ground · B1.A DIRECTORY LOCATION (DVR) ground · 4 E1.1 EB.1 OMIT STOP · 5 E9 · 6 E4 E7 · 7 E16 EB.2 E12.1 SHORELINE ground · B4.A OMIT · B1. OMIT · 8 E9 E13 · 9 E14 · B1.B DIRECTORY LOCATION (DVR) · 10 STOP NO MOTOR VEHICLES ground · 11 ground (DVR) · 12 E15 · 13 E6 E7

13.1 E1.1 EB.1 STOP ground

A1.A AREA IDENTITY SIGNAGE (DVR) ground

JUNIPER ROAD

- future LRT

COMMERCE BLVD

Public parking deck

Mixed Use

Retail

AUDITOR'S RD 40

AUDITOR'S ROAD DISTRICT

SHORELINE DRIVE

Lost Lake Harbor

NORTH

4'-10" SETBACK FROM BIKE TRAIL

10'-5" SETBACK FROM BIKE TRAIL 4'-0" SETBACK FROM SIDEWALK

19 E9 E13 ground · 20 E1B quantity: 2 ground · 21 E9 E13 concrete · 22 E4 E7 ground · B1.D DIRECTORY LOCATION (DVR) ground · 23 DRINKING FOUNTAIN (no sign needed) · 24 E11 LOST LAKE quantity: 2 ground · B1.E DIRECTORY LOCATION (DVR) · 25 E9 E13 ground · 26 E3 ONLY ONLY ground · 27 E9 E13 ground · 28 SHORELINE AUDITORS STOP E12 (x2) E1 EB ground

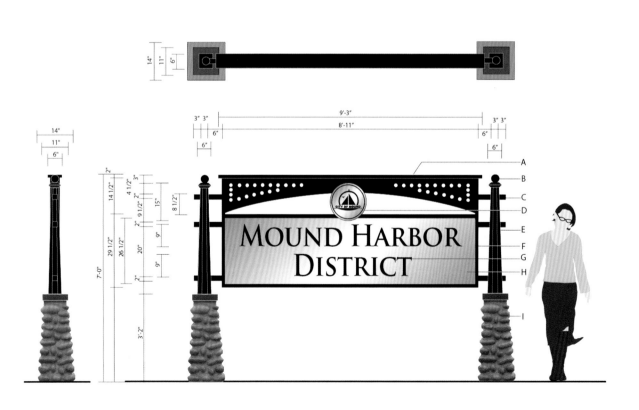

MOUND HARBOR DISTRICT

14" / 11" / 6"

9'-3" / 8'-11"

3" 3" / 6" / 6"

A B C D E F G H I

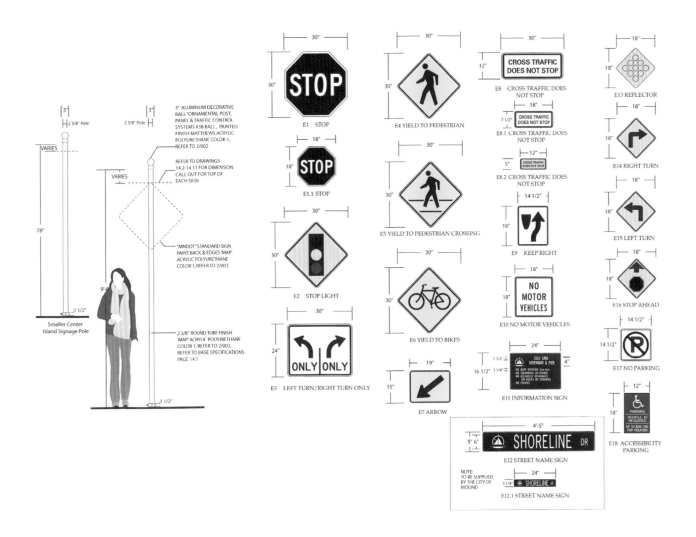

Smaller Center Island Signage Pole

3" ALUMINUM DECORATIVE BALL "ORNAMENTAL POST, PANEL & TRAFFIC CONTROL SYSTEMS #3B BALL", PAINTED FINISH MATHEWS ACRYLIC POLYURETHANE COLOR 1, REFER TO 2/002

REFER TO DRAWINGS 14.2-14.11 FOR DIMENSION CALL OUT FOR TOP OF EACH SIGN

"MNDOT" STANDARD SIGN PAINT BACK & EDGES 'MAP' ACRYLIC POLYURETHANE COLOR 1, REFER TO 2/002.

2 3/8" ROUND TUBE FINISH 'MAP' ACRYLIC POLYURETHANE COLOR 1, REFER TO 2/002, REFER TO BASE SPECIFICATIONS PAGE 14.1

E1 STOP
E1.1 STOP
E2 STOP LIGHT
E3 LEFT TURN / RIGHT TURN ONLY

E4 YIELD TO PEDESTRIAN
E5 YIELD TO PEDESTRIAN CROSSING
E6 YIELD TO BIKES
E7 ARROW

E8 CROSS TRAFFIC DOES NOT STOP
E8.1 CROSS TRAFFIC DOES NOT STOP
E8.2 CROSS TRAFFIC DOES NOT STOP
E9 KEEP RIGHT
E10 NO MOTOR VEHICLES
E11 INFORMATION SIGN

E13 REFLECTOR
E14 RIGHT TURN
E15 LEFT TURN
E16 STOP AHEAD
E17 NO PARKING
E18 ACCESSIBILITY PARKING

E12 STREET NAME SIGN
E12.1 STREET NAME SIGN

NOTE:
TO BE SUPPLIED BY THE CITY OF MOUND

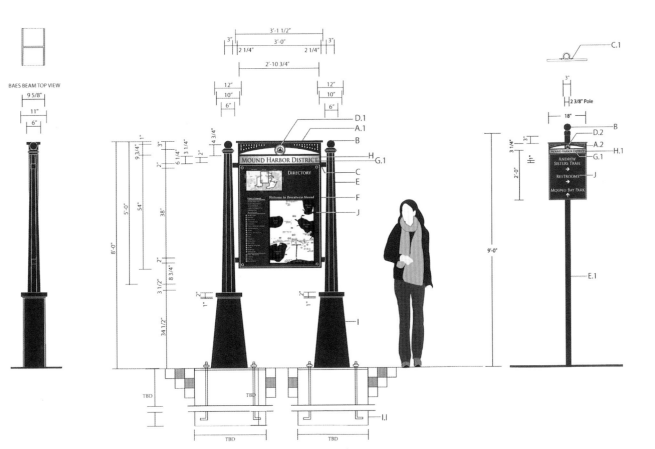

BAES BEAM TOP VIEW

MOUND HARBOR DISTRICT
DIRECTORY
Welcome to Downtown Mound

ANDREW SISTERS TRAIL
RESTROOMS
MOUND BAY PARK

Rapid Rail
Network in
Gauteng >>

For the last three years the team at Red Hand, Vista System's South African distributor, has been working closely with the Architects on the specification of the wayfinding signage for the Gautrain project. The project was installed successfully and in time for the FIFA World Cup 2010.

Vista System was the obvious choice for a project of this nature as it compliments the design & atmosphere in the Gautrain stations. Vista System is also the only MCFT (Modular Curved Frame Technology) System that could cover all signage aspects of the project using one system without having to use multiple systems from various vendors which streamlined the process.

Also of importance to the Architect was the fact that Vista System has been certified as GREEN and friendly to the environment.

Design Agency:
Vista System
Designer:
Vista System
Photography:
Vista System
Client:
The Gautrain
Location:
South Africa
Date:
2009

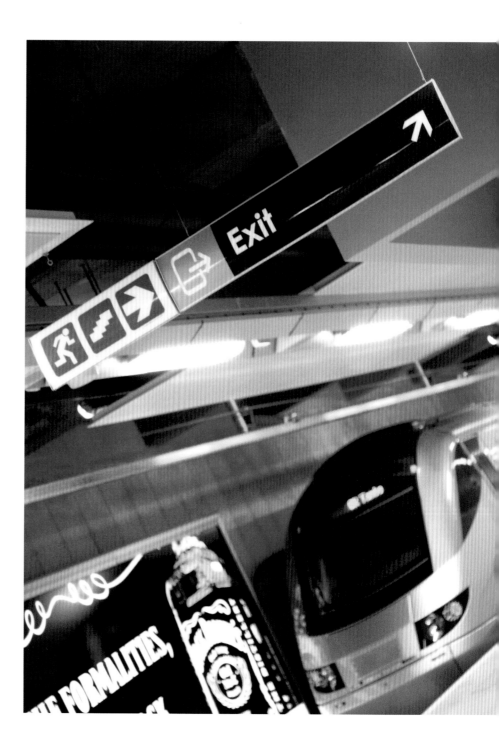

Naumburg Historical City Centre >>

The use of bright signal colours has been avoided in favour of a muted colour palette. The idea is for pedestrians to find information, but not to be swamped with information as in an airport. With this in mind, the following design elements were developed: so-called info bedstones are used at central guide points. They aid spatial comprehension visually and haptically, since they mark the location and reflect the city's ground plan in a stylised manner. Streets, squares and public areas are shown recessed (approximately 3 to 5 millimetres). Particular landmarks of the city (for example the cathedral and other sacred buildings) are marked in bronze. The circular info bedstones (2.20 metres diameter) are manufactured from reinforced, frost-resistant, free-flowing, high-performance fine-grained concrete. The info mast, 2.50 metres high and with tablet-shaped extension arm, marks the visitor's location in the city's ground plan, and also serves as an information board. The mast is made of a cylindrical aluminium tube with flat decorative head and sits firmly, pointing north, in a ground sleeve also made of aluminium. An aluminium sign measuring 30 x 150 centimetres is inserted in a guide slot and can be locked.

Design Agency:
Meuser Architekten GmbH
Photography:
Miriam The designersber
City of Naumburg S.
Client:
City of Naumburg S.
Fachbereich Stadtentwicklung
Bau
Location:
Germany
Date:
2007

Metallschild
Format 30 x 150 cm

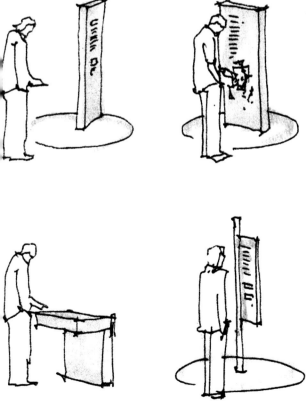

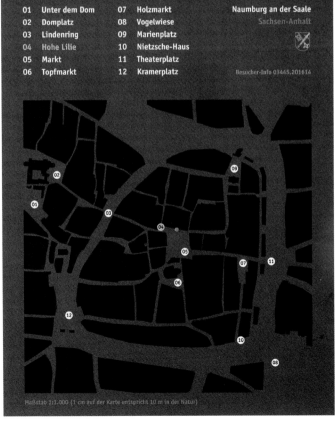

01	Unter dem Dom	07	Holzmarkt
02	Domplatz	08	Vogelwiese
03	Lindenring	09	Marienplatz
04	Hohe Lilie	10	Nietzsche-Haus
05	Markt	11	Theaterplatz
06	Topfmarkt	12	Kramerplatz

Naumburg an der Saale
Sachsen-Anhalt

Besucher-Info 03445.201614

Maßstab 1:1.000 (1 cm auf der Karte entspricht 10 m in der Natur)

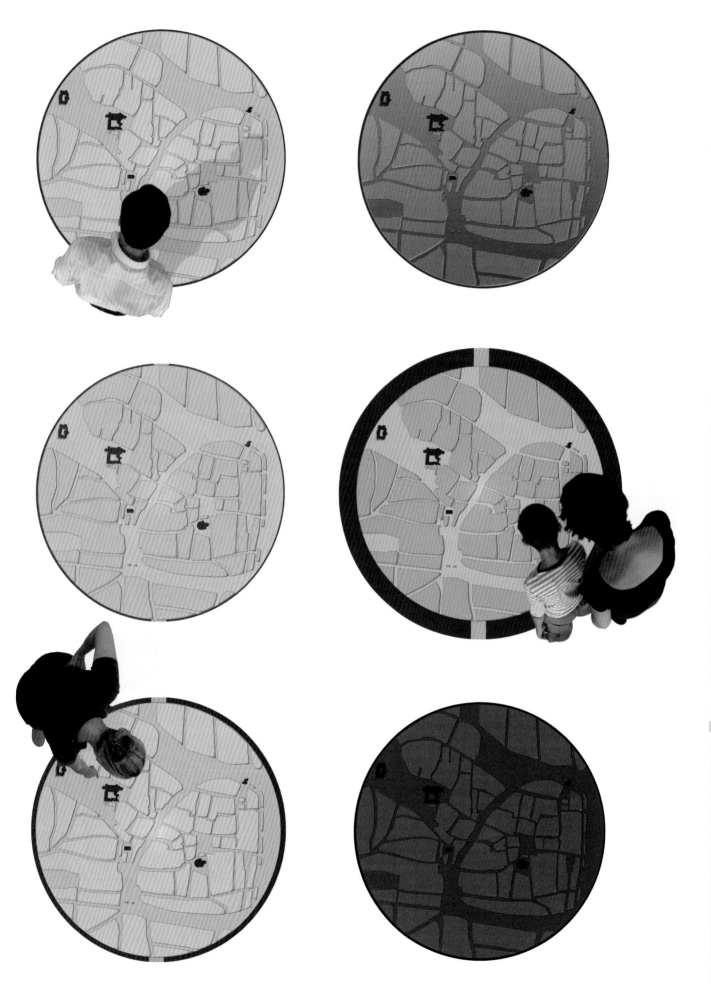

Graphic Design in Architecture: Where Image Meets Information

Over the past forty years, signage and environmental graphic design have evolved from tasks that were primarily functional to a design discipline that is increasingly recognised as an aesthetic that enhances how people experience the built environment.

Design begins with research and analysis, to fully understand the client's intent, strategies, and objectives for all kinds of projects, whether interior systems, urban wayfinding, or interpretation and guidance for recreational trails in wilderness. Wayfinding, interpretive and placemaking concepts guide, announce, inform, celebrate, and even warn people, serving many functions in many different environments. Graphics help express both the character and intent of a project.

For example, increasingly, offices have become important expressions of a company's brand, communicating its mission not only to employees, but to all who come to do business with it.

Shopping centres seek to establish an attractive character, whether urban upscale luxury, suburban lifestyle centres, or big box discounting.

The designer must anticipate all the decisions a visitor must make, often in an unbuilt project, ranging from a complex transportation system providing directions, identifications of routes, stations, schedules, etc. or a healthcare facility where effective graphic design serves the dual purpose of wayfinding and reassuring patients and visitors who may already feel anxious.

Large crowds at stadiums and sports events find their seats, their hot dogs, and their memorabilia with the help of graphic systems operating at many levels.

Patience, vision, and collaborative skills are prerequisites for signage designers faced with projects that may run several years or experience long pauses, based on the various stages of work the architects must complete before signage and wayfinding can be completed.

Those early stages of audit and analysis are key phases and the odds for success rise significantly when the signage and wayfinding designers are brought onto the team early in the overall process. Beginning with the kick-off meeting, it is critical to start a dialogue establishing parameters for everything from the physical characteristics of the site to the brand image as well as the budget constraints.

Designers programme locations of signs, the necessary information, and how each message is worded. They design the look and feel of the typography, colours, structure, materials, lighting and how each sign type is integrated into the built environment.

The wayfinding designer analyses routes and orientation methods for users to navigate a project. Often the questions designers ask in trying to establish nomenclature (naming), as well as informational and directional messages, can help both client and architect clarify the operational intent of areas of a project.

Research, programming, schematic design, design development and prototyping, construction documentation, bid support and construction administration are all parts of the scope of services environmental graphic designers provide their clients but every project is unique and the specific methods are dictated by the needs of the situation.

Typically, exterior and interior categories of signage are compiled into a comprehensive message schedule, coupled with location plans that identify all decision points and consider the sign types necessary to deliver the message – for example, does the information need to be illuminated or not? Should it be overhead, freestanding, or wall mounted, etc.? Is dynamic or changeable information required at this location? – all decisions to be made before a single sign is designed.

Typography, symbols and maps are the vocabulary of wayfinding systems. The fonts selected carry the personality and image of the project expressed in every message.

Using fonts that are clear and legible the signage designer has to logically prioritise information. Messages are often viewed from a distance by both pedestrians and vehicular passengers, and graphic information in a three-dimensional environment behaves significantly differently from the printed page of a book or magazine.

Typefaces designed with a large x-height (lower case letter), medium stroke width and medium character width are going to be more legible than those without. Equally important are letter spacing and line spacing.

Messaging and typography need to mesh with materials and three-dimensional design, again requiring collaboration between disciplines. Forms and textures relating to the architecture and interiors transform type into environmental graphic design.

Sculptural forms, thoughtful choice of materials, and detailing that relates to the environment, perform a delicate balancing act that complements the architecture while enhancing its purpose – whether it's placemaking, wayfinding, interpretative design or even donor recognition.

Susan Chait

Lebowitz | Gould | Design, Inc.

SA Water House >>

For the new SA Water House development in Adelaide, the designers developed a major signage and environmental graphics scheme as part of the interior fitout and building design. The primary objective of the development is to unite all facilities and staff into one site, encouraging interaction and teamwork. The design approach was based on water, using the water-pipe as a metaphor for connection, and referencing cylinders, circles and translucency throughout the extensive signage package. The encompassing design solution adds depth and dynamism to the SA Water head office reinforcing its position as a lead agency in the water industry. Internally, the designers created a varied palette for staff to respond to and be inspired by. The signage and graphics guide users through the space and aim to educate and entertain. SA Water's 150 years history is introduced with timeline rods forming the backdrop to the main reception desk. Overall the graphics retain natural light and views through the workspaces, emphasising openness and encouraging interconnections. The designers also created two major placemaking features – a super-scale graphic on the building façade and reception glazing, and massive 25-metre-long river graphic applied to custom-woven stainless steel mesh hanging in the Atrium.

Design Agency:
Frost design
Client:
South Australia Water
Location:
Adelaide, Australia
Date:
2009

The Toy Manufacturing Company Schleich >>

The Toy Manufacturing Company Schleich is well known for its very detailed animal figures, which it sells all over the world. This company, from Baden-Wuerttemberg, set the task of developing an information and guidance system which would fit in with the corporate identity created by the Landor branding agency. Furthermore, the new extension on the company's premises also had to be integrated into an overall concept with regard to the new guidance system. The requirement furthermore consisted in guiding the daily visitors, and the more than 200 employees through the complex buildings over the shortest possible route, while also diverting the deliveries transport widely around the neighbouring residential area. The smallest modular unit, the circle (as a two-dimensional representation of the ball), forms the core of the pictorial language developed. Buildings that are functionally separated are coded accordingly by colour and a relevant animal. At the intersections, spheres with three-dimensional overview plans offer information on the location. In addition, coloured animal tracks with distance information guide visitors through the buildings as if they were on trails. The specially-designed pictograms in their basic form are also based on the spot. The creative focus was on harmonising the interior design with the design concept and the colour spectrum of the signage. Thus, animal motifs form a trail through the new offices and impart a playful lightheartedness to the otherwise austere offices.

Design Agency:
Meuser Architekten GmbH
Architecture:
Schöne • Seeberger • Müller
Freie Architekten BDA
Photo Credits:
The designersrner Huthmacher
Client:
Schleich GmbH
Location:
Baden-Wuerttemberg, Germany
Date:
2010

2.143

Jörg Müller
Lager und Anlieferung

3.201

Katrin Grunewald
Marketing und Vetrieb

A_01.015

Paul Kraut
Geschäftsführung

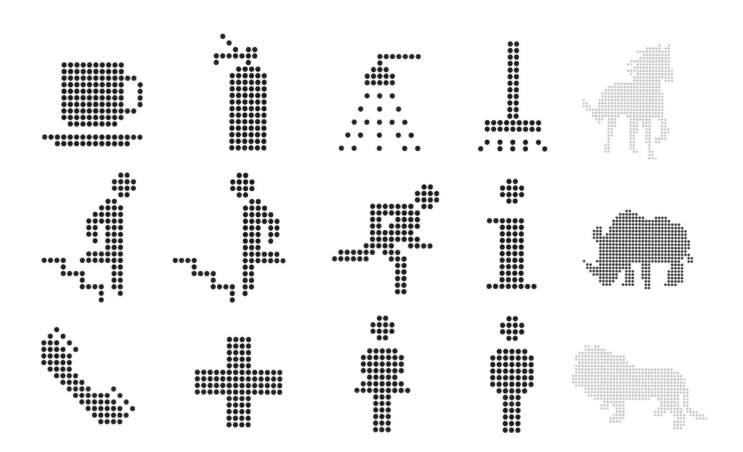

ABS 1001

Cremeweiß
Art-Nr. 03335500

Taubenblau
Art-Nr. 03255500

Gelb
Art-Nr. 03338300

Rostrot
Art-Nr. 03252700

DTAC House >>

"DTAC house" is the new office of DTAC, Thailand's second largest mobile network operator, located in Chamchuri Square, Bangkok. The interior design uses wood texture and straight lines as main elements, with a clean and sleek mood. In order for the signage system to blend in with the interior design, the designers choose wood textured strips as the key element and find the right size and width by studying all the details, like the height of the cabinets along the main pathway. To keep the friendliness and warmth of the DTAC brand image, they designed the pictograms to be very simple with minimum lines and detail and use them along side the DTAC (Telenor) corporate typeface, despite the fact that the client gave the designers total freedom to choose any typeface they found appropriate.

Design Agency:
Conscious
Creative Director:
The designerse Viraporn
Designer:
Chatnarong Jingsuphatada
Nathida Wongmahasiri
Photography:
Pirak Anurakyawachon
The designerse Viraporn
Client:
DTAC
Location:
Thailand
Date:
2009

premium

lounge

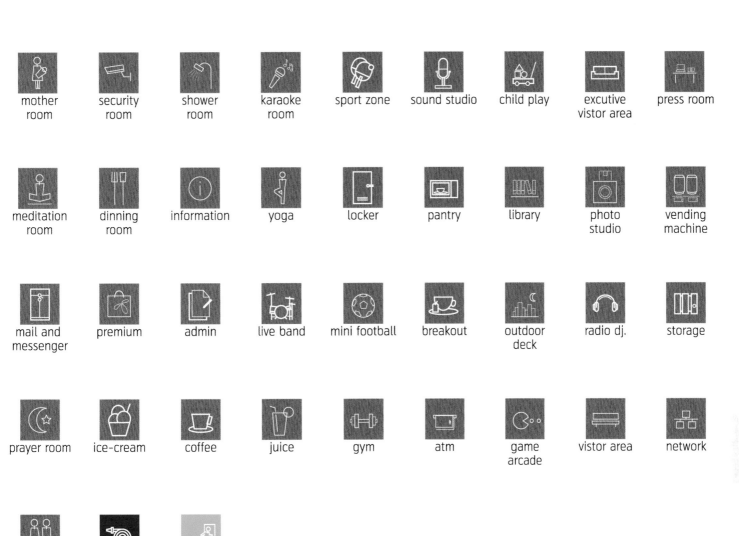

mother room	security room	shower room	karaoke room	sport zone
sound studio	child play	excutive vistor area	press room	

meditation room	dinning room	information	yoga	locker
pantry	library	photo studio	vending machine	

mail and messenger	premium	admin	live band	mini football
breakout	outdoor deck	radio dj.	storage	

prayer room	ice-cream	coffee	juice	gym
atm	game arcade	vistor area	network	

toilet	fire hose	fire exit

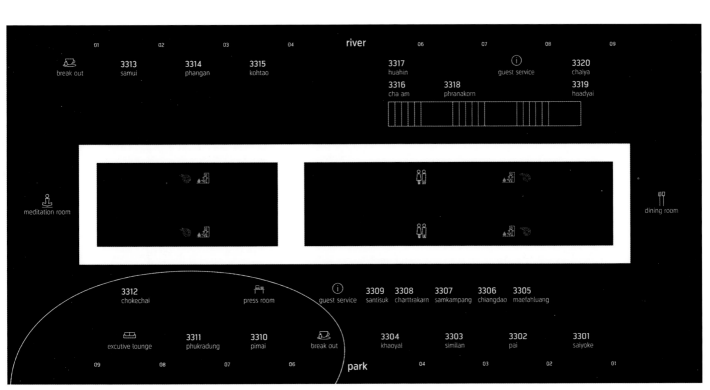

01　02　03　04　river　06　07　08　09

break out
3313 samui　3314 phangan　3315 kohtao　3317 huahin　guest service　3320 chaiya
3316 cha am　3318 phranakorn　3319 haadyai

meditation room

dining room

3312 chokechai　press room　guest service　3309 santisuk　3308 charttrakarn　3307 samkampang　3306 chiangdao　3305 maefahluang

excutive lounge　3311 phukradung　3310 pimai　break out　3304 khaoyai　3303 similan　3302 pai　3301 saiyoke

09　08　07　06　park　04　03　02　01

service hall

mail

break out

L144 –
The
Foundry >>

The logo, which was redesigned when the building underwent full restoration, is based on a casting of a sign showing details of the area's history in chronological order. The main motif for the building's sign system consists of a collage of signs and stamps which used to be produced in the foundry. Specially developed pictograms provide visitors with quick and easy orientation and point out important facilities such as the toilets, lifts, entrances and exits.

Design Agency:
Naroska Design
Photography:
Rudi Meisel
Client:
L144
Location:
Germany
Date:
2008

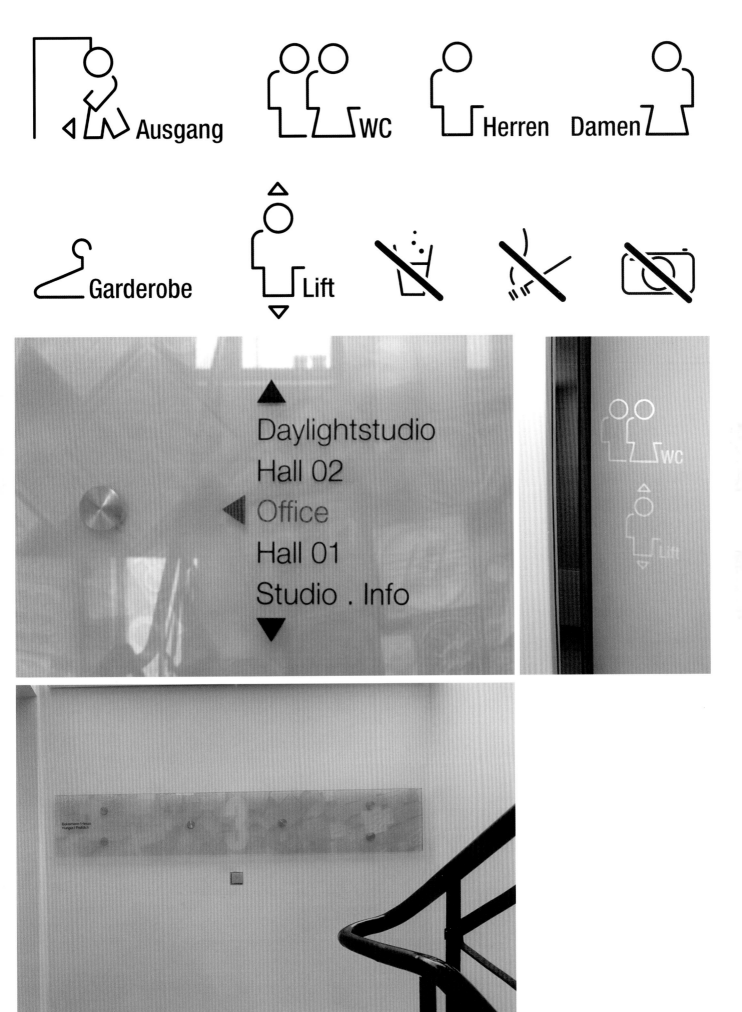

◁ Ausgang

WC

Herren   Damen

Garderobe

Lift

Daylightstudio
Hall 02
◀ Office
Hall 01
Studio . Info

WC

Lift

Mirvac
Western
Australia >>

Mirvac WA's new office is an inspired, engaging and hospitable environment to do business. Geyer created the interior and worked with BrandCulture to bring the brand into context throughout the environment. This was important for the employees at Mirvac, after being re-branded and relocated, keeping the culture strong was paramount to the company. The office required an independent identity, whilst remaining true to the Corporate Brand.

The "living line" (a Mirvac branding device used to connect all aspects of the company's business) had been used in the Sydney office to great effect and again formed the backbone to this branded environment albeit in an edgier, more graphic form. BrandCulture saw the line connecting the floorplate's central meeting room hub with the satellite meeting locations in the office as the perfect metaphor reflecting the Perth office's relationship within the organisation. Mirvac's Head Office is situated on the eastern seaboard in Sydney, while the Perth office is situated 4000 kilometres on the western seaboard. This "connectivity" is one of the cornerstones of the Mirvac brand messaging, so it made sense to establish this in a graphical context.

Design Agency:
BrandCulture
Creative Director:
Stephen Minning
Design Director:
Antonijo Bacic
Photography:
Stephen Minning
Client:
Mirvac Group
Location:
Perth, Australia
Date:
2009

3:08
BINNINGUP BEACH

Mirvac
Sydney >>

Working in collaboration with geyer, BrandCulture created a branded environment that is an impressive setting for visitors and clients. The "Living Line" concept, previously used in Mirvac's marketing collateral and internal communications, became the linking theme for graphic elements across the office, creating continuity throughout and emphasising the scope and diversity of the brand. Staff areas feature a vibrant and colourful environment, stimulating employees and encouraging active engagement with the brand.

Colours and graphics individually selected for each floor act as an orientation reference. From the building's core, it is difficult to orientate, therefore "core plinths" were positioned displaying the rising and setting sun. The sunrise located on the eastern side of the building and the sunset on its west, communicate the Mirvac brand story of a strong history and a commitment to a sustainable future. The complete environment includes six floors at 60 Margaret Street, in Sydney's CBD. It creates a compelling and architecturally focused environment to embody the mission and values of this iconic brand.

Design Agency:
BrandCulture
Creative Director:
Stephen Minning
Designer:
Antonijo Bacic
Photography:
Stephen Minning
Client:
Mirvac
Location:
Sydney, Australia
Date:
2009

Sydney
Water
Parramatta >>

The core concept for this project with Sydney Water encapsulates the company's recent resettlement; "the journey to Parramatta" is a visual narrative of Sydney Water's history from Australian white settlement to the present day and its commitment to safe water supply. With this project, it was the wayfinding and graphical language defined by the system, that determined the look and feel of the interior graphical treatment. The journey begins on the ground floor building lobby and ends on the Level 16 breakout floor. The naming convention for the meeting rooms tie into the journey, taking inspiration from bays and parks that correspond with significant locations along the Parramatta River. Each floor lift lobby features a graphic representation of a river section with blue vinyl lines floating down the wall. The graphic language devised for the building also extended into the statutory signage requirements, which needed to conform with building codes and regulations, while being compatible with architectural finishes. This resulted in a bespoke designed icon library and well considered placement and typography. Formed Polypropylene signs in the shape of a droplet, (mirrored in the lift lobby directory boards) were created for tactile requirements, and durable photo anodised aluminium selected for the public areas of the building.

Design Agency:
BrandCulture
Creative Director:
Stephen Minning
Design Director:
Antonijo Bacic
Designer:
Terry Curtis
Photography:
Studio Commercial
Client:
Brookfield Multiplex
Location:
Perth, Australia
Date:
2009

Parramatta Park

The indigenous inhabitants were the Burramatta ('burra' meaning eel and 'matta' meaning creek) clan of the Dharug people. In 1788 Governor Phillip chose Parramatta Park as the second settlement of New South Wales.

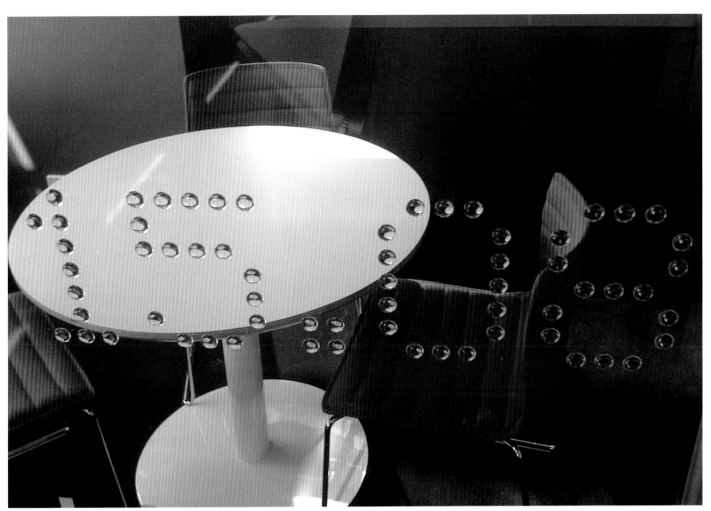

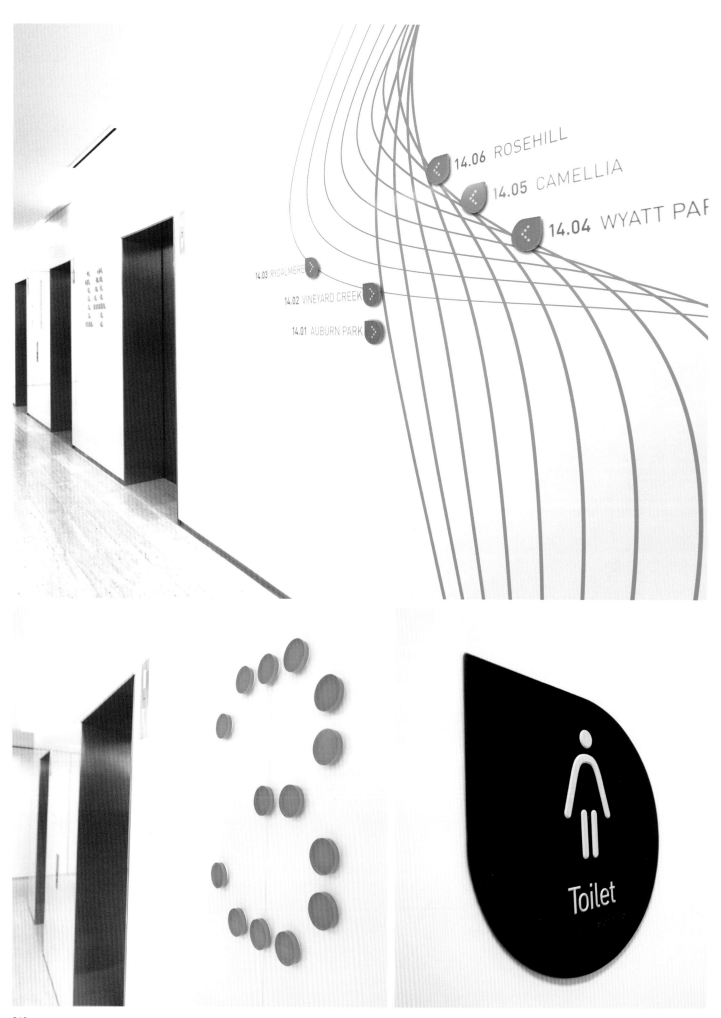

14.06 ROSEHILL

14.05 CAMELLIA

14.04 WYATT PAR

14.03 RYDALMERE

14.02 VINEYARD CREEK

14.01 AUBURN PARK

Toilet

10.01 Silverwater Park
10.02 Kissing Point Bay
10.03 Yaralla Bay
10.04 Majors Bay
10.05 Merrylands Bay
10.06 Olympic Park
10.07 Breakfast Point

11.01 Homebush Bay
11.02 Meadowbank
11.03 Brays Bay
11.04 Rhodes Park
11.05 Powells Creek
11.06 Liberty Grove
11.07 West Ryde
11.08 Concord West
11.09 Strathfield
11.10 Eastwood

12.01 George Kendall Reserve
12.02 Melrose Park
12.03 Alrey Park
12.04 Bressignton Park
12.05 Boronia Park
12.06 Sumerville Park
12.07 Dence Park

8.08 W ELIZABETH BAY

DARLING POINT

OTTS POINT

MORNE POINT

Office of Chief Medical Examiner Forensic Biology Laboratory >>

It is a comprehensive exterior and interior sign programme for this state–of–the–art forensic facility.The programme includes unique wayfinding requirements and special signage for bio-chemical laboratories, handling and storage.

Design Agency:
Lebowitz|Gould|Design, Inc.
Creative Director:
Ed Frantz
Photography:
Lebowitz|Gould|Design, Inc.
Client:
Perkins Eastman
Architects, PC
Location:
USA
Date:
2007

Bio Chemistry
Immuno/Histo Chemistry
ISN/GL Evidence

Suite 706

Quality
Assurance

Suite 610

Post-Amplification Labs
Molecular Genetics Labs
RNA Diagnostics

Floor 7

Steiner
Studios >>

It is a distinctive identification and wayfinding programme for the largest film production studio complex on the east coast. The industrial themed signage identifies the five sound stages with accompanying offices, shops, freight, catering and support services on a 15-acre site in the Brooklyn Navy Yard.

Design Agency:
Lebowitz|Gould|Design, Inc.
Creative Director:
Sue Gould
Photography:
Ruggero Vanni/Vanni Archives
Lebowitz|Gould|Design, Inc.
Client:
Steiner Studios
Dattner Architects
Location:
USA
Date:
2006

One Raffles Quay >>

At over 185,800 square metres, One Raffles Quay is among Singapore's largest office tower developments. It consists of two towers, a car park, a retail arcade, and multiple connections to the subway and pedestrian bridge systems. C&VE designed the dramatic site identification signs and all core and shell signs for the mammoth complex.

There are two sculptural site identification signs: one of hand crafted cast glass letters, and the other of laminated glass letter forms inlaid into stone panels and rear illuminated. Illuminated totem signs of stainless steel and custom-made pattern glass provide orientation and identification information. Illuminated overhead signs provide easy directions.

Design Agency:
Calori & Vanden-Eynden / Design Consultants
Art Director:
David Vanden-Eynden
Designer:
David Vanden-Eynden
Chris Calori
Denise Funaro
Photography:
Tim Nolan
Client:
Hong Kong Land Ltd.,
Keppel Land International Ltd.,
Chueng Kong (Holdings) Ltd.
Location:
Singapore
Date:
2007

Hearst
Corporation
Head-
quarters >>

The Hearst Corporation has created a new landmark in Manhattan by taking their 1928 Art Nouveau building and adding a 44-storey steel and glass tower designed by Foster + Partners. The inside of the historic building is now a single, 2-metre-high sky-lit atrium space. The challenge was to design a sign programme that would integrate into both the original building and the minimalist modern tower rising above it. The solution is a system of freestanding "totems" made out of glass and stainless steel that serve many necessary functions. In addition to identification and directional information, the totems house the lobby's security cameras and the call buttons for a sophisticated lift system. The rest of sign programme keys off the totem design with typefaces chosen to relate to the corporate identity of the Hearst organisation. The tower graphics make use of a wealth of graphic identity inherent in the magazines that are part of the Hearst family.

Design Agency:
C&G partners
Partner-in-Charge:
Keith Helmetag
Lead Designer and Project Manager:
Amy Siegel
Photography:
David Sundberg
Chuck Choi
Client:
Hearst Corporation
Location:
USA
Date:
2007

Grey
Group >>

A creative company needs an innovative workspace. For Grey Group, one of the largest marketing communications companies in the world, a move to a new, state-of-the-art headquarters in the Flatiron District, a New York design centre, symbolised a renewed commitment to creativity.

Scher and Studios previously collaborated on the interiors of the Bloomberg L.P. headquarters, where Scher developed an environment of numbers that was a three-dimensional manifestation of the Bloomberg brand. For Grey, Scher has designed graphically playful signage that captures and promotes the creativity of the company's various divisions. The programme utilises materials used in the interior design to create a series of optical illusions that brand the agency in the space. "It's a house of visual games," says Scher.

Studios designed the interiors using different materials for each division or department on each floor. Scher's environmental graphics use these same materials – wood, glass, metal and polymer – in ways that suggest the personalities of the different divisions. The signage mixes the materials with elements of reflection, transparency, lighting and pattern to create a series of optical illusions that sets each department apart and at the same time ties the headquarters together into a cohesive environment.

Design Agency:
Pentagram
Art Director:
Paula Sche
Designer:
Paula Scher
Andrew Freeman
Client:
Grey Group
Location:
USA
Date:
2009

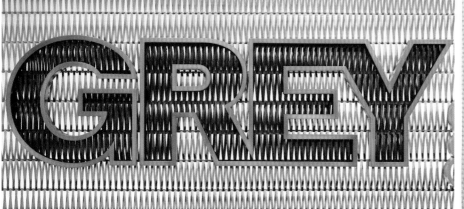

MYER
Office >>

MYER, Australia's largest department store recently relocated their head office to Docklands.

BVN Architects commissioned Buro North to design graphic embellishments and signage throughout the space.

After a thorough research phase, the designers crafted design which evolves throughout the nine floors; each floor is themed by a specific decade in the twentieth century fashion, starting with the 1910s and working up through the building to the 1990s.

Wall Graphics were relief routered and signage developed using a feature material relevant to the decade; toilet pictograms were given the same decade relevant treatment creating a subtle and sophisticated interpretation of MYER's heritage.

Design Agency:
Buro North
Designer:
Soren Luckins
Dave Williamson
Jules Zaccak
Sarah Napier
Tom Allnutt
Photography:
Peter Bennetts
Client:
BlighVollerNeild (BVN)
Location:
Australia
Date:
2010

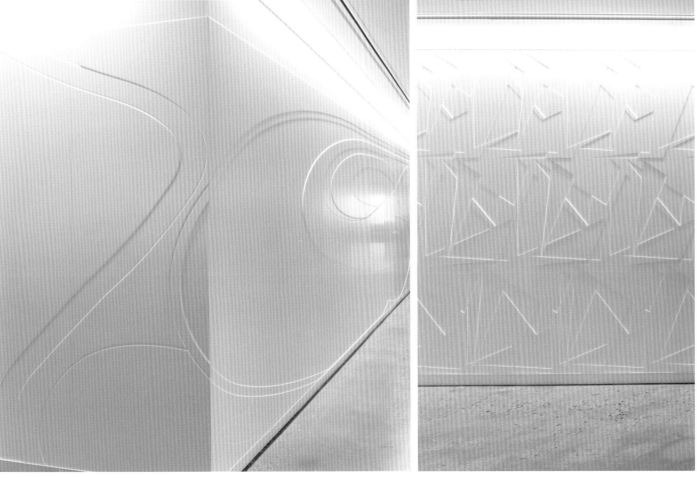

2101
L Street >>

Located just four blocks from the DC metro, the new 5,574-square-metre, LEED-CI Platinum office is a shining example of a next-generation sustainable corporate interior. The design team began with an extensive immersion process to better understand the client's culture and work processes. From the immersion process, five core types of spaces, or "activity zones" emerged – Greet, Seat, Meet, Eat and Retreat – each representing different components of how the office functions. A major challenge – and accomplishment – was creating environmental graphics that were sustainable or had sustainable elements while being extremely durable and long-lasting. The resulting environmental graphics elements met the needs of the client and end-user by enhancing the modern, creative and cutting-edge space with a fully-integrated environmental design that simultaneously stays mindful of the client's sustainable goals.

Green materials include sustainable adhesives for the wall coverings, finishes for wall plaques and overhead signing, material selection for large-scale graphics, collateral materials such as personal metal water canteens to reduce waste, low energy use digital rotating bulletin board announcements to convey office-wide accomplishments and information, as well as magnetic bulletin boards throughout the office to reduce office paper distribution and consumption.

Design Agency:
RTKL Associates Inc.
Photography:
David Whitcomb
Anne Chan
Paul Warchol
Client:
RTKL Associates Inc.
Location:
USA
Date:
2008

The
Monarch >>

Soaring 300+ feet skyward over the West End/Market District at the western edge of Austin's Central Business District, The Monarch is a trend-setting example of smart growth that will redefine Austin's downtown skyline. Austin is known for its Monarch butterflies, which pass over the city during their annual migration to Mexico. Renowned throughout the natural and human worlds as creatures of significant beauty and grace, the Monarch inspired RTKL to design a space that similarly pays tribute to the ideas of natural beauty and international intrigue. When translated to design, this concept took the form of a 29-storey high-rise tower with sleek, clean lines that radiate European efficiency while maintaining an earthy, Austin feel through judicious use of natural materials and colours. Other interesting design references include the glass handrail system, which creates a pixilated effect reminiscent of Monarch wings, and a Monarch-shaped roof detail that crowns the building. Rounding out The Monarch experience, RTKL's graphic design team created marketing brochures that expanded the concept and communicate a cohesive experience.

Design Agency:
RTKL Associates Inc.
Photography:
David Whitcomb
Client:
Bellevue Square
Location:
USA
Date:
2008

TAP >>

The design approach started simultaneously with the wayfinding system and the chromatic study of the building. The concept for the wayfinding system started from the Dada movement. Words and letters are freely arranged and partially expressed in an onomatopoeic way. The building is literally a container for words and sounds.

"TAP", the name of the building, is comprised of the initial letters of "Théâtre et Auditorium de Poitiers" and is supposed to refer to the three taps in the beginning of a play. The guidance system consists of oversized letters and numerals recognisable from a wider distance. The colours used are a continuity of the building colours, black and yellow.

To announce the events of each season were developed the guidelines for the exterior video projections in the glass "skin" of the building, like a deconstructed video screen with moving images.

An exterior signage system consisting of "totems" in the surroundings of the building, is the limit of the design project.

The technical solutions for all the applications are painting with moulds, and adhesive film directly in the walls and other surfaces in order to avoid three-dimensional elements.

Design Agency:
P-06 ATELIER
Art Director:
Nuno Gusmão
Creative Director:
Nuno Gusmão
Estela Pinto
Pedro Anjos
Designer:
Vera Sachetti
Giuseppe Greco
Miguel Cochofel
Miguel Matos
Photography:
Sérgio Guerra SG+FG.
Client:
JLCG Arquitectos
Location:
France
Date:
2008

The California Endow- ment >>

A lively and thoughtful new headquarters for the California Endowment's "Centre for Healthy Communities" has taken root on a once dilapidated industrial site in downtown Los Angeles. The graphics work began with the development of a refreshed and stronger logotype, expressive of the Endowment's newly expanded, multilayered nature. The system of interior and exterior identity icons and wayfinding signage reflect the strong bold colours of architecture. Freestanding digital directories inside the lobby doors and digital screens at the meeting rooms communicate the changing daily meeting and conference information through an instantly adjustable, paperless system.

Design Agency:
Sussman/Prejza & Co., Inc.
Creative Director:
Deborah Sussman
Holly Hampton
Designer:
John Johnston
Hsin-Hsien Tsai
Ana Llorente Thurik
Selene Gladstone
Photography:
Jim Simmons
Client:
The California Endowment
Location:
USA
Date:
2006

cafe

Mammoth

Mojave

6 Catalina

Lansing

Yahoo! >>

Yahoo! hired Square Peg to design a creative and memorable monument identity incorporating the Yahoo! logo and a signing and graphic programme to inform and direct visitors throughout the five-building corporate headquarters. In 2002, Square Peg Design received the Merit Award from the Society of Environmental Graphic Design (SEGD) for work on the Yahoo Campus.

Design Agency:
Square Peg Design
Creative Director:
Scott Cuyler
Designer:
Scott Cuyler
Photography:
Square Peg Design
Client:
Yahoo!
Location:
USA
Date:
2006

Wayfinding or Wayshowing?

"There is no one perfect orientation system for a building or site!" is a statement that we always come up with in the very first meeting with a new client. It has to become clear in their mind that the ways of orientation are as individual as their users, needs and background.

The concept and design of a signage system has always got a lot to do with the political attitude of the initiator/principal. Someone has to decide how dominant it should or should not be?

To achieve adequate solutions we design a variety of media for the following different ways of orientation:

1. The ideal way to guide: From human to human – the quality of personal assistance is irreplaceable by any sign or screen. Individual needs can be answered in a personal dialogue.

2. The haptic way to guide: Miniature representations of the original. Through miniature scale models huge dimensions can become immediately clear as well as visitors' positions and destinations.

3. The transportable way to guide: Printed maps for take-away. Maps are leading visitors along their path.

4. The common way to guide: Signs and screens.

Now, guiding system design is considered as a key element in the overall success in the design of modern public place. Museums, schools and other cultural public places need appropriate guiding system. Those early stages of audit and analysis are key phases when the signage and wayfinding designers are brought onto the team early in the overall process. Every project is unique and the specific methods are dictated by the needs of the situation, and thus the key is to set accurate information on the exact location, and give an expression through an accurate and unified visual language. The stages of audit and analysis refer to the existing signage system, the types and backgrounds among the audience, place classification, the visiting routes, flow direction, and the architectural style and colour, etc. An in-depth survey could help choosing and optimising the guiding system information reasonably, providing an accurate basis for the design. Design is an implementation of the guiding system on the basis of the survey, including the choice of the colour and the secondary colour, the definition of the icons, system specifications, map design, product design guides, interesting ideas, information centre or touch screen design.

During the design of the museum guiding system, the designers need to get an in-depth research on the built environment, including the constant discussion with the architects and the museum's sponsor, the pedestrian routes, separation and guidance, partition and numbering, etc. Usually, we need to learn from other excellent museums in the world, and make much improvement according to the characteristics of local culture. Form design is more challenging, designers need to balance the sense of history and the way of information reception as well as the differences in the international reading habits; let the design not only reflect the importance of the museum, but also integrate into the strong and minimalist modern environment. Each step needs to be discussed and checked repeatedly, the sense of mission and responsibility accompanies with the designer all the time.

Museums as one of the public utilities, its self-positioning is clearly different from the commercial area, so in the museum guiding system, besides the prerequisites guides, office guides, public guides, the more important is the visiting services guides, and how to do it well has turned to be a key element in the building of the personalised, comfortable and relaxing space.

Campus guiding system design needs to balance the historical and cultural resources as well as the innovative environment of space, give full considerationto the participatory, artistic quality and functionality of the public art installations in the campus environment and thus creates reasonable specification-oriented system. It is an integral part of modern university landscape. It is the core of shaping a new image of the campus culture. The designers need to get an in-depth research on the built environment, geographical layout and traffic routes and the interior departmental structure of the administrative office building, teaching building, public school buildings, student apartment buildings, public spaces and other construction sites as well as the pedestrian traffic routes and so on. The analysis of the campus environment from outside to inside could benefit the classification and the grading of the design.

Campus guiding system is an important part of the scenic design in the campus. To shape a unique brand image of the campus culture, the design needs to sum up the history of the school, refining the inner spirit and the educational philosophy, to visualise and systematise the spirit and cultural heritage, to combine the community's awareness on campus and the school's own sense, to develop, refining, nurture and shape the historical heritage of the spiritual qualities.

Christopher Ludwig

founder of F1RSTDESIGN

Zeche
Zollverein >>

Zeche Zollverein is an abandoned coal mine in Essen which has been listed as UNESCO World Heritage site in 2001. Following a masterplan of OMA/Rem Koolhaas from 2002 the whole area is developing into an important centre for culture and design. Zollverein accomodates such institutions as museums (i.e. red dot design museum) , over 100 companies, several event locations and a design school. The design intention is to create a signage system without conventional signs. It is conceived to guide with minimal yet distinctive clues rather than confusing by installing a forest of signs. It introduces a great variety of tools such as personnel, 3D cast iron miniature models, ground markings, lightened panels as well as printed media in a combination of low-tech and high-tech methods. From a miniature representation of the original, the visitors find miniature scale casting iron 3D models of the complete area at all entrances. The huge dimensions become immediately clear as well as the visitors' positions and destinations. Chimneys and high buildings help to get an overview – Zollverein has a unique topography. The challenge of the wayfinding is to answer the needs of 500,000 visitors a year while at the same time cope with the strict regulations of the monument conservation.

Design Agency:
F1RSTDESIGN
Photogarphy:
F1RSTDESIGN
Client:
Zeche Zollverein
Location:
Ruhrgebiet, Germany
Date:
2010

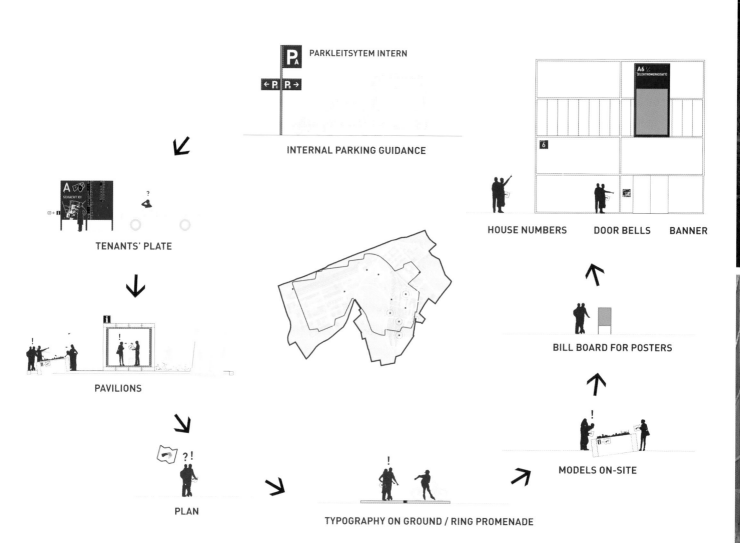

PARKLEITSYTEM INTERN

INTERNAL PARKING GUIDANCE

TENANTS' PLATE

PAVILIONS

PLAN

TYPOGRAPHY ON GROUND / RING PROMENADE

HOUSE NUMBERS   DOOR BELLS   BANNER

BILL BOARD FOR POSTERS

MODELS ON-SITE

PERIPHERY

ENTRANCE

TENANTS' PANEL

RECEPTION: WELCOME...!

AREA   RING PROMENADE   AREA   DESTINATION

A [ELEKTROWERKSTATT]
6

[ZENTRALWERKSTATT]
5

Glasgow
Science
Centre >>

Glasgow Science Centre comprises three distinctive buildings – the Science Mall, an IMAX Theatre (Scotland's first) and the Glasgow Tower. The area is vast and to guide visitors around its layers, BDP Design, London, were commissioned to create a communication system, including signage, which would reflect the spirit of the unusual structures as well as providing clear guidance information to visitors.

The designers deliberately made finding the way around an integral part of the Centre's exploration process. At the same time the signage enhanced the identity of the Centre whilst providing a strong element of consistency against which individual attractions could stand out.

Design Agency:
BDP Design
Creative Director:
Richard Dragun
Designer:
Richard Dragun
Lynda Athey
Photogarphy:
David Barbour
Client:
Glasgow Science Centre
Location:
Glasgow, UK
Date:
2010

Parcours Des Rescapes >>

This Scenographic promenade is a centennial of a mining disaster, Courrières on March 10th 1906. Along a 1.5 kilometre route the designers created a unique visual language. The design of signage supports and various scenographic elements solemnly reveal the identity of the site. Besides the mission of informing to remember and understand, they are placed respectfully on the site, facilitating the transmission of memory. According to the sequences of the route, these visual elements are like a land-art intervention. The fight of the survivors during twenty-one days in the restricted space of the galleries is related on twenty-one easels.

Designer:
Nicolas Vrignaud
Jean-Marc Louazon
Landscaper :
TERRITOIRES SITES ET CITÉS
Architects & Landscapers
Client:
CALL
Location:
France
Date:
2006

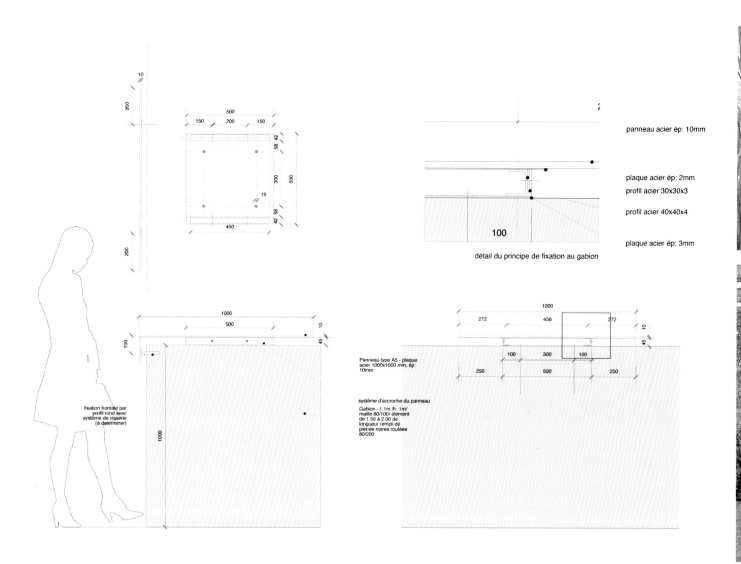

panneau acier ép: 10mm

plaque acier ép: 2mm

profil acier 30x30x3

profil acier 40x40x4

plaque acier ép: 3mm

détail du principe de fixation au gabion

fixation frontale par
profil rond avec
système de visserie
(à déterminer)

Panneau type A5 - plaque
acier 1000x1000 mm, ép:
10mm

système d'accroche du panneau

Gabion - l: 1m /h: 1m/
maille 80/100/ élément
de 1.50 à 2.00 de
longueur rempli de
pierres noires roulées
80/200

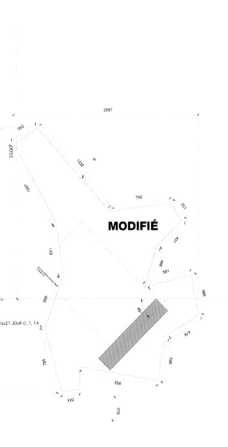

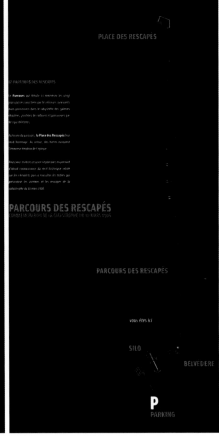

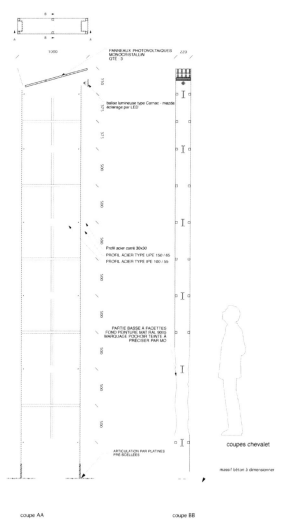

coupe AA   coupe BB

FANNEAUX PHOTOVOLTAIQUES
MONOCRISTALLIN
QTÉ : 3

balise lumineuse type Carnac - mazda
éclairage par LED

Profil acier carré 30x30
PROFIL ACIER TYPE UPE 150 / 65
PROFIL ACIER TYPE IPE 100 / 55

PARTIE BASSE À FACETTES
FOND PEINTURE MAT RAL 9005
MARQUAGE POCHOIR TEINTÉ À
PRÉCISER PAR MO

ARTICULATION PAR PLATINES
PRE-SCELLÉES

coupes chevalet

massif béton à dimensionner

MERCREDI 14 MARS 1906 _ Jour 5

L'atelire
Cultural
Centre >>

This project is a hommage to the old shops signs, still existing in some towns or villages. The designers made a selection of the fonts mainly used to write the information. The designers added an external sign for the entrance, a 4-metre-high type sculpture with light encrusting in the steel skin.

Designer:
Nicolas Vrignaud
Architect :
AAVP architects
Client:
Ville de Gournay en Bray
Location:
Gournay en Bray, France
Date:
2010

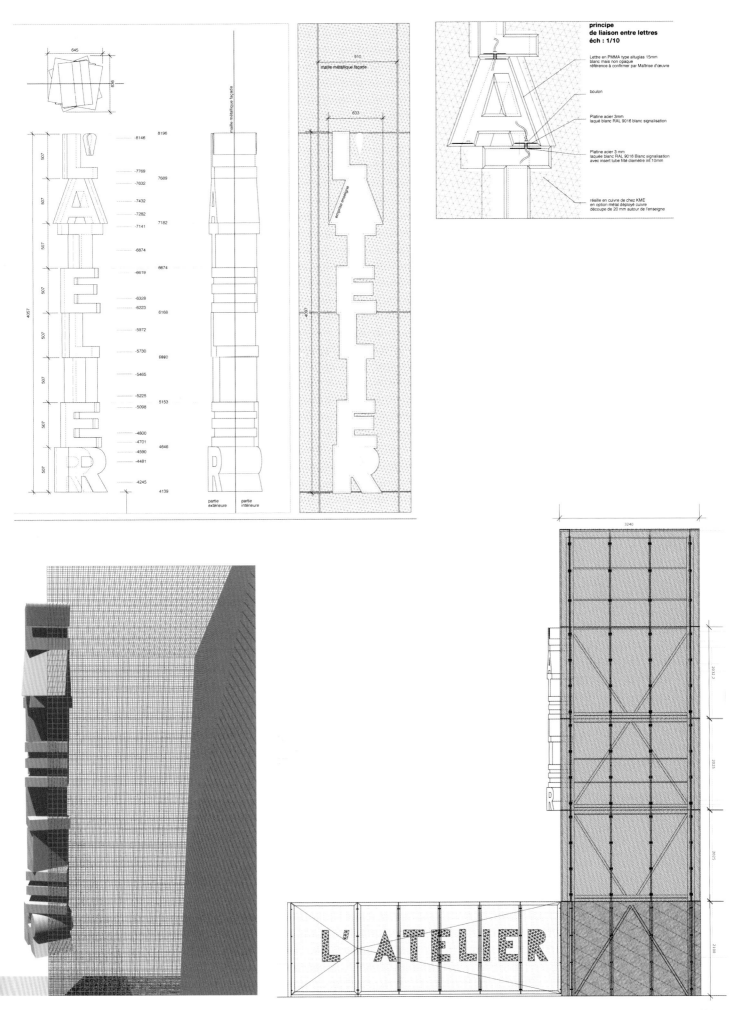

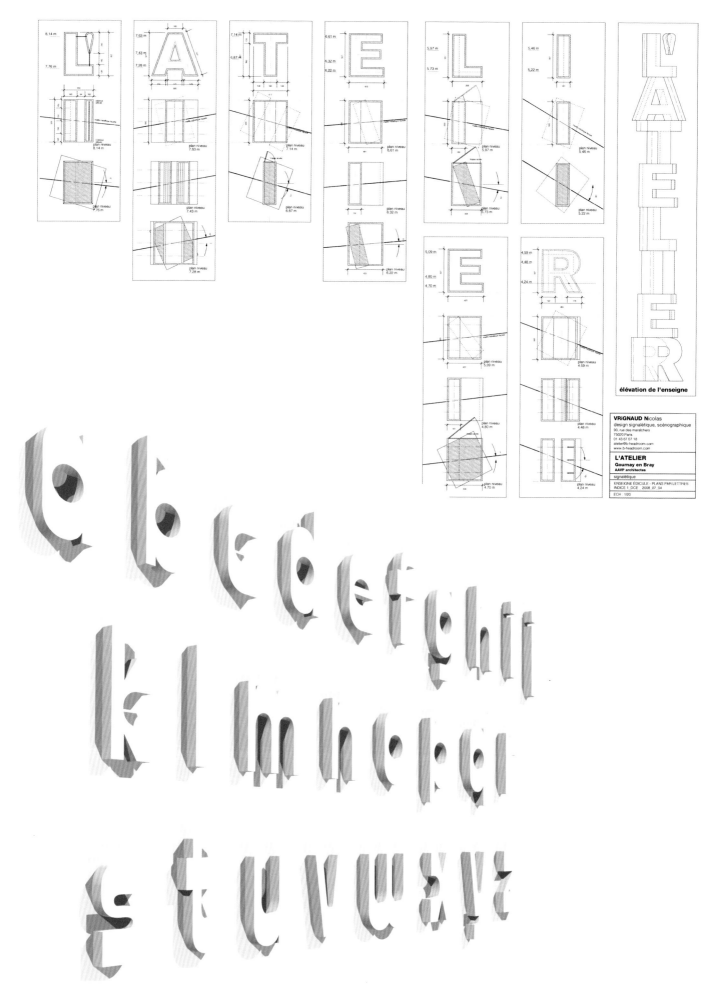

élévation de l'enseigne

VRiGNAUD Nicolas
design signalétique, scénographique
90, rue des maraîchers
75020 Paris
01 43 67 07 18
atelier@b-headroom.com
www.b-headroom.com

L'ATELIER
Gournay en Bray
AAVP architectes

signalétique

ENSEIGNE ÉDICULE - PLANS PAR LETTRES
INDICE 1 DCE   2008 07 04

ECH   1/00

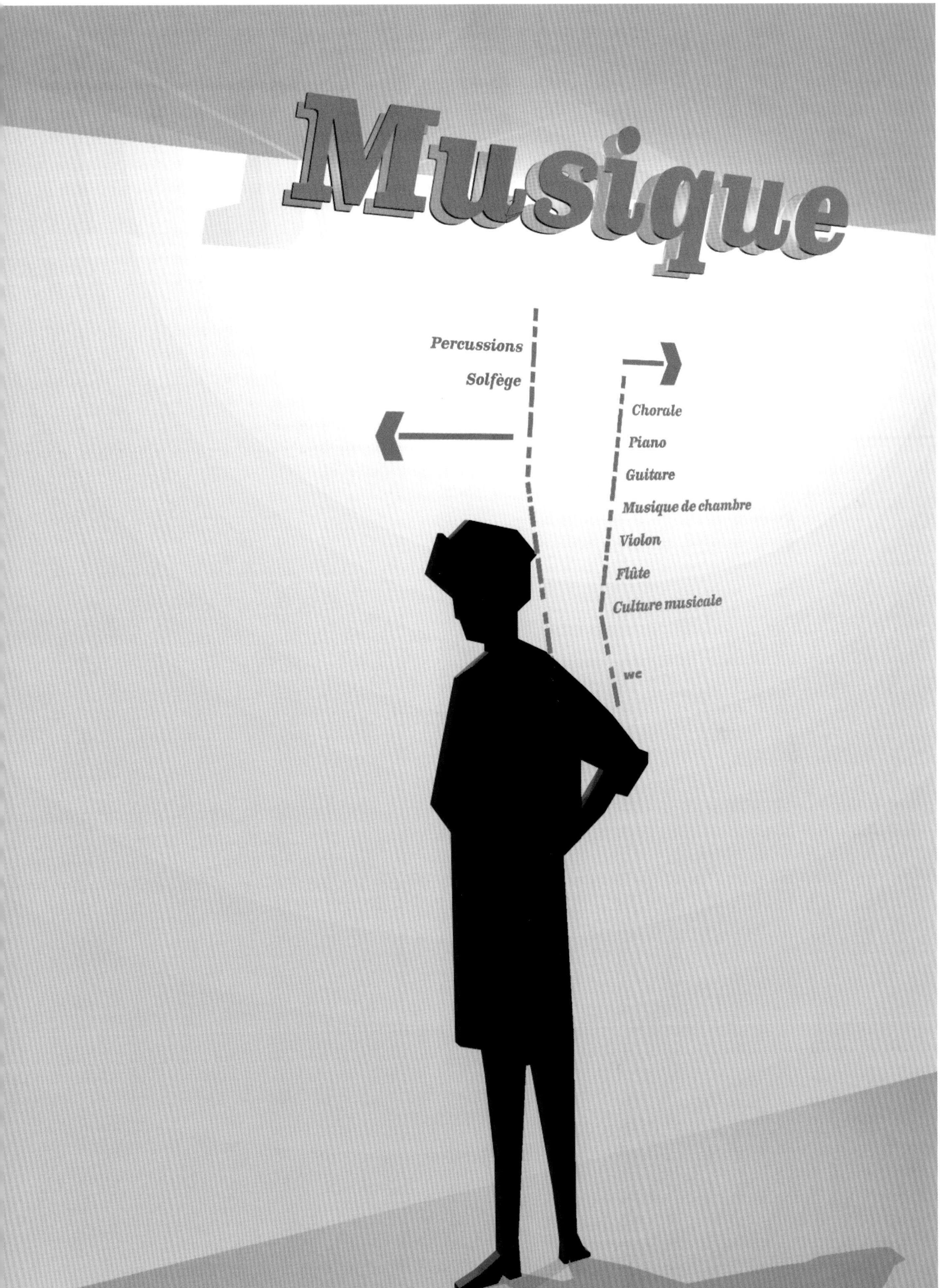

Musique

Percussions

Solfège

Chorale

Piano

Guitare

Musique de chambre

Violon

Flûte

Culture musicale

wc

Schomburg Centre for Research in Black Culture >>

It is a comprehensive signage programme for renovation and expansion of the Schomburg Centre, one of the specialised research libraries of the New York Public Library. The curtainwall building identification is a custom interlayer in glass which varies with the lighting conditions.

Design Agency:
Lebowitz\Gould\Design, Inc.
Creative Director:
Alper Yurtseven
Photography:
Ruggero Vanni/Vanni Archives
Lebowitz\Gould\Design, Inc.
Client:
NYC DDC
Dattner Architects
Location:
USA
Date:
2009

Divus
Vespas-
ianus >>

It is a visual identity for an archeological exhibition on the Roman emperor Vespasianus (the founder of the Colosseo), made inside the Colosseo of Rome.

Design Agency:
Tassinari/Vetta
Art Director:
Leonardo Sonnoli
Client:
Archeological Board of Rome
Electa Publishing House
Location:
Italy
Date:
2010

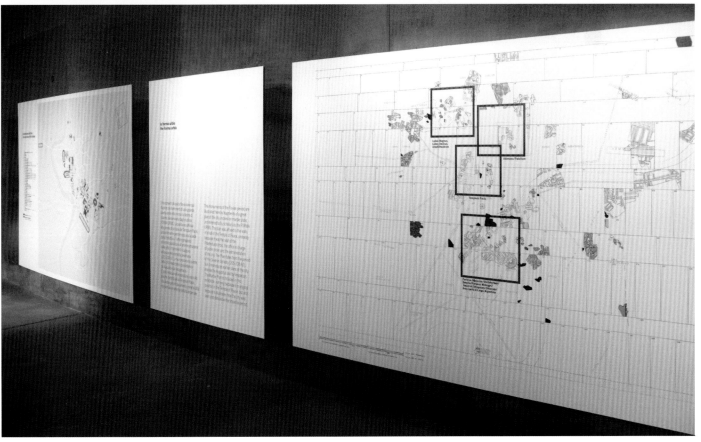

Imp. T. Caesari/Divi f./Vespasiano Aug./
Plebs Urbana/quae frumentum/
publicum accipit/et tribus [XXXV]

Le distribuzioni di grano alla plebe
"All'imperatore Tito Cesare, figlio del Divo Vespasiano,
la plebe urbana che ha ricevuto il grano pubblico, e le
35 tribù."

Le due iscrizioni gemelle, provenienti probabilmente
entrambe dall'area dell'Arco di Tito, documentano il rin-
graziamento della plebe urbana, ossia delle 35 tribù in
cui era suddivisa, per le distribuzioni gratuite di grano
fatte da Tito. Nell'area dovevano infatti trovarsi gli Horrea Vespasiani, con la probabile funzione di magazzini
per il grano.

The distribution of grain to the plebs
"To the emperor Titus Caesar, son of the God Vespasian, the urban plebs who received the public grain, and
the 35 tribes."

These identical inscriptions probably came from the
area of the Arch of Titus. They record the thanks of the
urban plebs, and the 35 tribes into which they were di-
vided, for the free distribution of grain by Titus, in fact,
the Horrea Vespasiani, which probably served as the
warehouses for the storage of the grain were situated
in this area.

"Finalmente i Flavi raccolsero e consolidarono il potere reso a lungo instabile....
Questa famiglia era oscura e priva di memorie di antenati illustri, ma lo Stato non ebbe affatto a pentirsene."
Svetonio, Vita di Vespasiano, 1

"The empire, which for a long time had been unsettled... was at last taken in hand and given stability by the Flavian family. This house was ...obscure and without family portraits, yet it was one of which our country had no reason whatever to be ashamed."
Suetonius, The Life of Vespasian, 1

DIVUS VESPASIANUS

"...were...thrown down, that those bodies, all sought a form hacked in pieces, and finally that baleful, fearsome visage cast into the fire, to be melted down, so that from such menacing terror something for man's use and enjoyment should rise out of the flames."

Pliny the Younger, Panegyricus to the Emperor Trajan 52

La damnatio memoriæ

La damnatio memoriæ (letteralmente la cancellazione del ricordo) era un provvedimento di condanna, che privava la persona del proprio nome e della possibilità di trasmetterlo alla discendenza. Il Senato la decretava contro gli imperatori giudicati nemici dello Stato, e implicava la distruzione di tutte le immagini che li riproducevano e la cancellazione dei loro nomi dalle iscrizioni. Plinio il Giovane narra un momento della distruzione delle statue di Domiziano cui aveva assistito.

Damnatio memoriæ

The damnatio memoriæ was condemnatory (simply the erasing of remembrance), which deprived the person of the very name and of the possibility of passing it to their heirs. The Senate ordered it against emperors judged to be enemies of the State. It involved the destruction of all the images of this person and the erasing of their name from inscriptions. Pliny the Younger describes the event during the destruction of the statues of Domitian which he was present.

Tempe
Centre
for the
Arts >>

The Tempe Centre for the Performing Arts is one of the largest performing arts centres in the southwest United States. Designed by Barton Myers Associates, the building is a complex of multiple theatres housed under a much larger structure. The interior functions like a Main Street with side businesses.

AdamsMorioka designed the primary entrance sign to feel like two geographic forms had collided and were locked in place. The other graphic applications followed the same idea of geography and natural elements: air, earth, and water. Signage was applied to each building inside the centre to be seen across the desert landscape as a small village. Large, neon letterforms cast a different coloured glow onto the theatre and out into the desert night.

Design Agency:
AdamsMorioka, Inc.
Art Director:
Sean Adams
Noreen Morioka
Client:
Barton Myers Associates Inc.
Location:
USA
Date:
2006

080 THEATER
STAGE RIGHT

TEMPE CENTER
FOR THE ARTS

George Sim Community Centre >>

GNU Group worked closely with the project architect, Field Paoli, to design a complete sign system for this remodel and addition to a community centre in south Sacramento. The sign design solution tightly integrates with the overall architectural design approach.

Design Agency:
GNU Group
Art Director:
Tom Donnelly
Designer:
Chris Uy
photography:
Tom Donnelly
Client:
Field Paoli Architects
Location:
Sacramento, USA
Date:
2010

San Leandro Senior Community Centre >>

GNU Group worked closely with the project architect, Group 4 Architecture, to develop a complete sign programme for this new senior centre in this suburban San Francisco community. The sign elements embrace the building forms and materials to reinforce the overall design concept.

Design Agency:
GNU Group
Creative Director:
Tom Donnelly
Designer:
Chris Uy
Photography:
Tom Donnelly
Client:
Group 4 Architecture
Location:
USA
Date:
2010

Museum
of East >>

The task assignment included creating an orientation and guidance system, communication products such as books, tickets and merchandising as well as the design of the museum's opening campaign. In the exterior a huge gold ingot announces the museum and its contents. Due to the broad columns and the low ceiling height in the exhibition rooms, the colour choice was black so as to create the sensation of theatre scenery in which the actors are the objects. The communication project uses the glass surfaces as blotting pads with writings and coloured textures identifying the Asian countries represented. China/gold, Macau/red, Japan/silver, Timor/green, India/orange, etc., which simplify the visual decoding of the exhibition spaces. The wayfinding system in the building uses oversized graphics due to the passageway configuration of the building. Gold leaf for the exterior; Paint, adhesive film and PVC panels for the signage system and communication.

Design Agency:
P-06 ATELIER
Art Director:
Nuno Gusmão
Creative Director:
Nuno Gusmão
Designer:
Joana Prosérpio
Vera Sachetti
Giuseppe Greco
Miguel Cochofel
Miguel Matos
Clara Jana
Photography:
Sérgio Guerra SG+FG
Francisco Feio
Client:
JLCG Arquitectos
Location:
Portugal
Date:
2006

The McNay
Art
Museum >>

To celebrate their 50th anniversary, this San Antonio museum embarked on an ambitious plan to renovate and re-envision this vital regional institution. The original structure, a majestic 19th-century mansion, has been expanded with a new wing designed by acclaimed architect Jean-Paul Viguiers to host major travelling exhibits.

The firm was initially engaged to plan and design the comprehensive exterior and interior sign and donor programme for the new expansion. The commission was expanded to encompass a new institutional identity, graphic system and print programme, creating a unique balance and integration between state-of-the-art architecture, environmental graphics, wayfinding, and branding.

Design Agency:
C&G partners
Partner-in-Charge & Project Manager:
Keith Helmetag
Lead Graphic Designer:
Emanuela Frigerio
Lead Sign Planner and Designer:
Amy Siegel
Photography:
Chuck Choi
Client:
The Paratus Group
Location:
USA
Date:
2008

Sculpture Gallery ↘
Garden Level Galleries
Lecture Hall
Learning Centers
Restrooms

↙ Sculpture Gallery
Garden Level Galleries
Lecture Hall
Learning Centers
Restrooms

Experimental Media Performing Arts Centre >>

EMPAC, on the Rensselaer Polytechnic Institute campus in upstate New York, is a new $350 million facility that houses four concert halls, café, radio station, offices, artist-in-residence studios and gallery. This fast-track sign and donor recognition project was done in collaboration with Grimshaw and Davis Brody Bond Aedas Architects.

Design Agency:
C&G partners
Partner-in-Charge:
Keith Helmetag
Associate Partner & Lead Sign Designer:
Amy Siegel
Designer:
Mika Owens
Photography:
Chuck Choi
Amy Siegel
Client:
Rensselaer Polytechnic Institute
Location:
USA
Date:
2008

6 Mezzanine

→

Concert Hall
Parterre

Restrooms

↑

Main Lobby

Concert Hall
Balcony

Administration

5 Café

→

Concert Hall
Orchestra

Theater

Studios

Restrooms

↖

Main Lobby

Concert Hall
Balcony &
Parterre

Administration

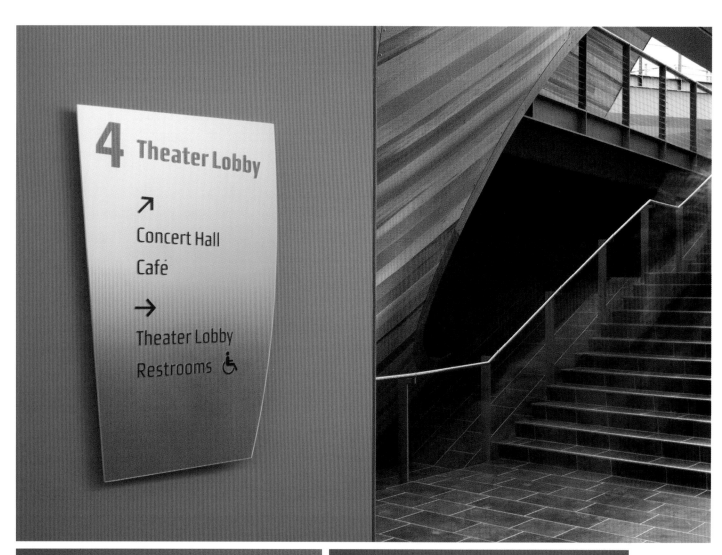

5 café
← Concert Hall
  Orchestra
  Theater
  Studios
  Restrooms

Two
Times >>

Two Times is a reflection on "It's about Time", achieved by means of a typographical intervention on an old hermitage's façade in Lisbon. The design goal was to attract new visitors to this art gallery. It presents titles relating to several themes taken from newspapers. A sense of humour and strangeness is encountered in phrases such as "Church recommends seven days of sex". At night, the façade is transformed into a huge light-box where the text is progressively separated from background by increasing its contrast and legibility. With the aid of a torch, it's possible to intervene on the installation.

Design Agency:
R2
Designer:
Lizá Ramalho
Artur Rebelo
Sign Planner:
Amy Siegel
Photography:
Fernando Guerra
Tiago Pinto
Client:
Hermitage Nossa Senhora da Conceição
em Belém
Location:
Portugal
Date:
2009

Ny
Carlsberg
Glyptotek >>

Ny Carlsberg Glyptotek was founded by the world-famous brewer, one of Denmark's largest patron of the arts. To coincide with its anniversary in 2006, the private art gallery created new presentations of its collection based on the notion of comprehension. The designers were hired to create a new signage system that would help make the collection more understandable to museum guests. Those who haven't been to a museum and have a sinking feeling would spend the next few hours wandering in perpetual confusion. The designers think it's at least in part because the sheer size and complexity of the organisation, layout and collection is immediately overwhelming. So for Glyptotek, the designers took that burden off the visitor, placing signs along the "relay-principle" – giving them just enough information to know where they are, what they're looking at, and how to get to the next sign. The signs are designed to complement the building's architectural features and the play of light and soft shadows on the works of art.

Design Agency:
Kontrapunkt
Creative Director:
Kontrapunkt
Designer:
Rikke Storm
Photography:
Rune Rasmussen
Client:
Ny Carlsberg Glyptotek, Copenhagen
Location:
Denmark
Date:
2006

**Lucius Verus, kejser
161-169 e.Kr.**

Fundet i Liciniernes grav i Rom.
Ca. 138 e.Kr. Marmor.

Lucius Verus bærer paludamentum, en
feltherrekappe. Portrættet er formentlig
udført i anledning af, at han i 138 e.Kr. blev
adopteret af kejser Antoninus Pius.

**Lucius Verus, Emperor
AD 161-169**

Found in the Licinian Tomb in Rome.
c. AD 138. Marble.

Lucius Verus wore the paludamentum,
a field commander's cloak. The portrait
probably dates to AD 138, the year of his
adoption by the Emperor Antoninus Pius.

En romer

Fundet i Liciniernes grav i Rom. Ca. 150-60
e.Kr. Marmor.

Den skæggede mand har nøgne skuldre.
Det viltre hår og krusede skæg er udført
med stor detaljerigdom. Han kan være et
medlem af Licinierfamilien fra 2. årh. e.Kr.

A Roman

Found in the Licinian Tomb in Rome.
c. AD 150-160. Marble.

This bearded man is shown with bare
shoulders. The tousled hair and curly
beard have been executed with a wealth of
detail. He may have been a member of the
Licinian family from the 2nd century AD.

National
Media
Museum >>

The designers have always believed that good design can make people's lives a bit easier, and sometimes it's simply the smallest detail that can have the biggest impact. What's important is the ability to listen and understand: to get under the skin of a problem and discover a solution that works, both on a functional and emotional level. Briefed to create a new wayfinding signage system for the National Media Museum in Bradford, the task was to improve visitor navigation around the complex and to ensure the system worked cohesively with the Museum's diverse range of exhibits. The new visual identity for wayfinding took its cue from the recognisable chevron shown repeatedly across film clapper boards. Bold typographic numbers and strong colours enable visitors to find their way through the complexity of the museum's many galleries, easily and quickly. The chevron motif was used across the museum: in isolation as moveable café signs, as a canvas for temporary exhibitions, and as a repeat pattern to guide visitors to the entrance and exits of the museum.

Design Agency:
Carter Wong Design
Designer:
Carter Wong
Photography:
Carter Wong
Client:
NMSI
Location:
UK
Date:
2009

FLOOR 7
CONFERENCE SUITE
Reserved access
LEARNING ROOMS
Reserved access

Woods Edge Community Church >>

Woods Edge is not an ordinary church. The phased masterplan includes a 8,360-square-metre worship facility located on 67 heavily wooded acres and features a 2,000-seat sanctuary. The design is modern and the designers wanted the graphics to reflect that. From the floating letterforms of the entry signage to the clean, flexible exterior and interior sign system the graphics mirror the client's vision of a modern place of worship.

Design Agency:
Formation
Creative Director:
David Hoffer
Philip LeBlanc
Designer:
David Hoffer
Philip LeBlanc
Erich Theaman
Photography:
Chan Do
Client:
Morris Architects
Location:
USA
Date:
2008

Worship Center
Children
First Time
Guests

Student
Ministry

Offices

WoodsEdge
COMMUNITY CHURCH

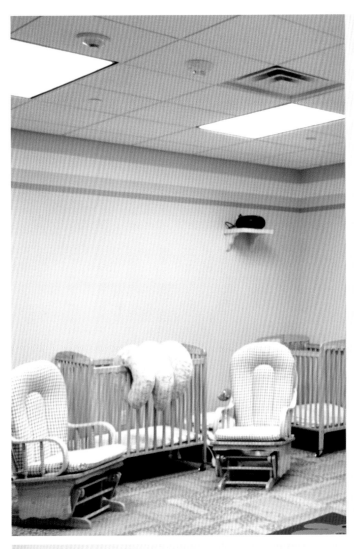

Infants
Tadpoles

wee
zone

0– 6 Months

102

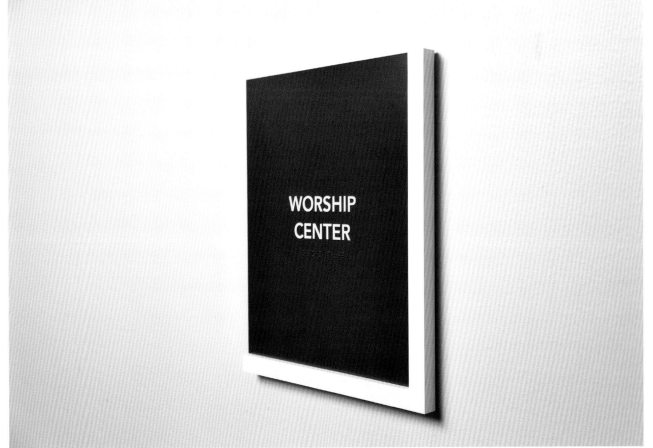

WORSHIP
CENTER

Australian
Museum >>

The Australian Museum, located in the centre of Sydney, is the oldest museum in Australia, researching and exhibiting natural history and anthropology. Originally founded in 1845, the museum has grown through the development of independent buildings connected by a central atrium space. Circulation through the museum's three public levels is not intuitive to the visitor. Lifts and stairs in the complex are not centrally located, sight lines are limited and reaching many important exhibits requires determined travel to isolated rooms. The wayfinding strategy was based on these fundamental principles: emphasise the central atrium as an arrival and orientation point; bring the qualities of the exhibits out into the public areas; use imagery that reflects the exhibits as universal information that also sparks curiosity; create a clear hierarchy of destinations where exhibits are dominant; express a visual personality rather than a neutral signage system; promote vertical travel within the museum using stairs and lifts.

Design Agency:
Dot Dash
Designer:
Mark Tatarinoff
Mia The designerssseling
Jonathan Rez
Photography:
Mark Tatarinoff
Client:
Australian Museum
Location:
Australia
Date:
2009

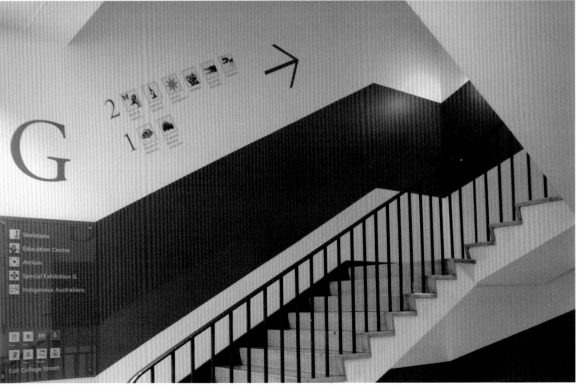

University of Green- wich >>

The Avery Hill Campus of the University of Greenwich provided an unusual wayfinding and information graphics project. At its centre is The Dome, housing a café and a large social space, which has been redesigned by architects Dannatt Johnson. For the signs and environmental graphics, the designers took the circularity of The Dome as their principal thematic idea. All the signs are pictograms reproduced on coloured circular discs to be used as the main identifiers for both directions and information. These discs are also used in a smaller, playful way on the glass surfaces of doors and windows. The room backgrounds have also been designed for the building with compositions of different sized, random-but-relevant large-scale words applied direct to the walls as digital prints. The words are used with different pacing to reflect the different uses of particular spaces and amplifying their personality and energy.

Design Agency:
Holmes Wood
Creative Director:
Lucy Holmes
Design Director:
Alex Wood
Photography:
Peter Cook
Client:
University of Greenwich
Location:
UK
Date:
2008

Achievement
First
Endeavor
Middle
School >>

With a little paint and some bold typography, a school designed to change the life of its students has undergone a transformation of its own. For the Achievement First Endeavor Middle School, a charter school for grades 5 through 8 in Clinton Hill, Brooklyn, Paula Scher has created a programme of environmental graphics that help the school interiors become a vibrant space for learning. The project was completed in collaboration with Rogers Marvel Architects, who designed the school as a refurbishment and expansion of an existing building. All of this was accomplished with little expense. As every homeowner knows, paint can be a simple and economical solution for transforming a space. At Endeavor the process required thorough planning. Using the existing colour palette, Scher and her team applied the colours to a scale model of the school to conceive of the patterns and placement for specific installations. In rooms like the cafeteria, the bands of colour are used to define and enhance the architecture, creating an illusion of depth that expands the space. In other areas, the painting of typography, set in Rockwell, is intricate and detailed.

Design Agency:
Pentagram Design
Designer:
Drea Zlanabitnig
Client:
Achievement First Endeavor Middle School
Location:
USA
Date:
2010

EDUCATION = ACCESS

EDUCATION = CHOICE

EDUCATION = POSSIBILITY

EDUCATION = FREEDOM

WHATEVER IT TAKES

MANY MINDS ONE MISSION

The
Cooper
Union >>

Cooper Union for the Advancement of Science and Art opened its new academic building on its Cooper Square campus in New York's East Village. Abbott Miller has designed a unique programme of signage and environmental graphics for the building that is fully integrated with the building's dynamic architecture.

For the signage typography Miller chose the font Foundry Gridnik, which resembles the lettering on the façade of the Foundation building. The original signage has a strong, angular look that suggests art, architecture and engineering.

The environmental graphics were also inspired by some of Miller's typographic explorations in his book *Dimensional Typography*. The signage typography has been physicalised in different ways, engaging multiple surfaces of the three-dimensional signs, appearing extruded across corners, or cut, extended and dragged through the material. The lobby of the new building is a soaring sky-lit atrium that rises up nine storeys through the building's core and is dominated by staircases. A dramatic installation recognising major donors animates the underside of a descending stairwell, the signage comprised of over eighty "blades" that cascade down the underside of the stairs, echoing the stairs' downward motion. The typography is engraved on the front, bottom and reverse surface of each blade.

Design Agency:
Pentagram Design
Designer:
Jeremy Hoffman
Brian Raby
Susan Brzozowski
Client:
Cooper Union
Location:
USA
Date:
2009

GEORGE AND MARY CAMPBELL CONFERENCE ROOM

FACULTY

...RTIN TRUST '56 AND DIANE TRUST

...ACQUES AND NATASHA

...AN TRUST

...FAMILY FOUNDATION,

...OWMENT

Southbank Institute of Techno-logy >>

Southbank Institute of Technology is the largest technical and further education college in Queensland. The 4-hectare campus has undergone a major refurbishment which included eleven new buildings and four refurbishments completed over a four year period. The design of the new site wide, wayfinding signage system responds to both the new corporate identity as well as other urban elements including street furniture.

Design Agency:
Dot Dash
Designer:
Domenic Nastasi
Photography:
Domenic Nastasi
Client:
John Holland Group
Location:
Australia
Date:
2008

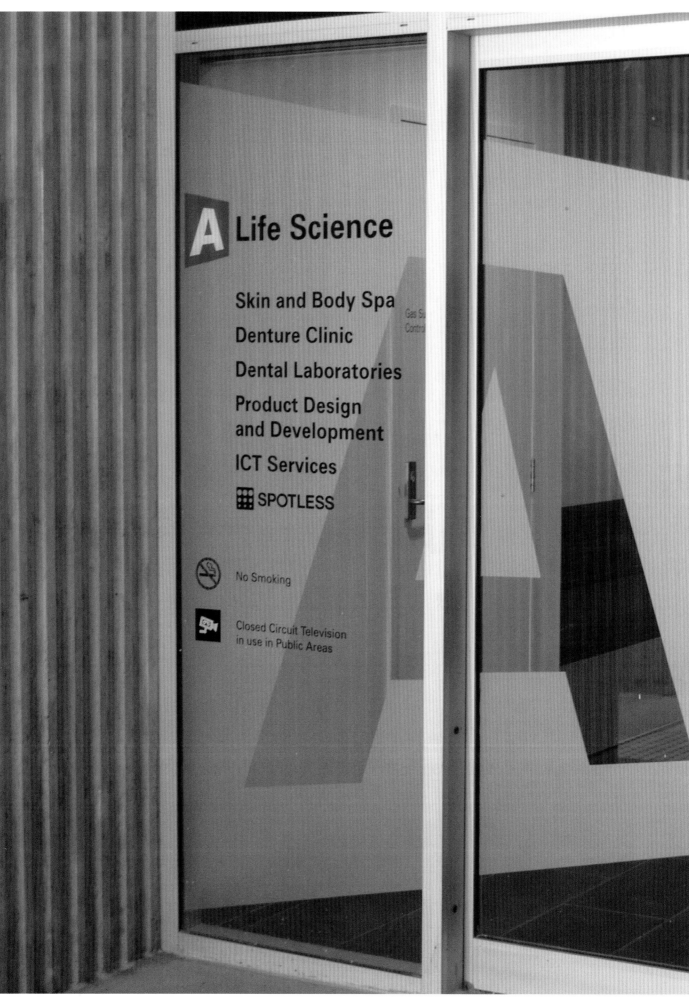

A Life Science

Skin and Body Spa

Denture Clinic

Dental Laboratories

Product Design
and Development

ICT Services

SPOTLESS

No Smoking

Closed Circuit Television
in use in Public Areas

Culcheth
High
School >>

The spatial design concept for Culcheth High School is a multi-level, linear street with three-storey "fingers" of transformational learning spaces. The fingers are joined by social hubs, which contain dining and conference facilities as well as Information & Communications Technologies and Learning Resource Centre. These are united by a "street", which links all the spaces together, providing a sense of place and community where learning can be seen and experienced.

Graphics and wayfinding provide the school with a strong brand message that at the same time, is warm, friendly and fun. Full height wall graphics of school "heroes" (including Brunel, Shakespeare, Martin Luther-King and Marie Curie) enforce the school's guiding principals of excellence. A strong wayfinding strategy using pictograms and colours underlines the brand whilst providing recognisable and identifiable areas as well as memorable markers to complement the signage scheme.

Design Agency:
BDP Design
Creative Director:
John Beswick
Designer:
Paul Atkins
Photography:
David Barbour
Client:
Canada's National Ballet School
Location:
UK
Date:
2009

Inclusion

S
1
S.1.12 - S.1.20

Sports

C
0
C.0.01 - C.0.19

English

S
0
S.0.02 - S.0.10

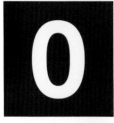

University College Dublin Library >>

University College Dublin Library required a comprehensive wayfinding signage system to guide 20,000 students through the library's four floors. Following a complete site evaluation seven signage classes were devised. Each of the four floors is now colour-coded to aid navigation. All new signs are designed to maximise legibility and meet all accessibility requirements. The new designs are also fully bilingual. The new signs establish a unified and consistent visual language system, benefiting all of the library's users. This project proves that thoughtful design can make a real difference.

Design Agency:
BFK
Creative Director:
Aiden Kenny
Designer:
Marie Vahey
Client:
University College Dublin Library
Location:
Ireland
Date:
2008

Léitheoirí Micreafoirm
Microform Reader

Printéir
Printer

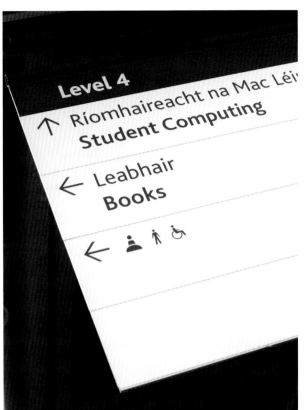

Level 4

↑ Ríomhaireacht na Mac Léi
Student Computing

← Leabhair
Books

← 🚧 🚹 ♿

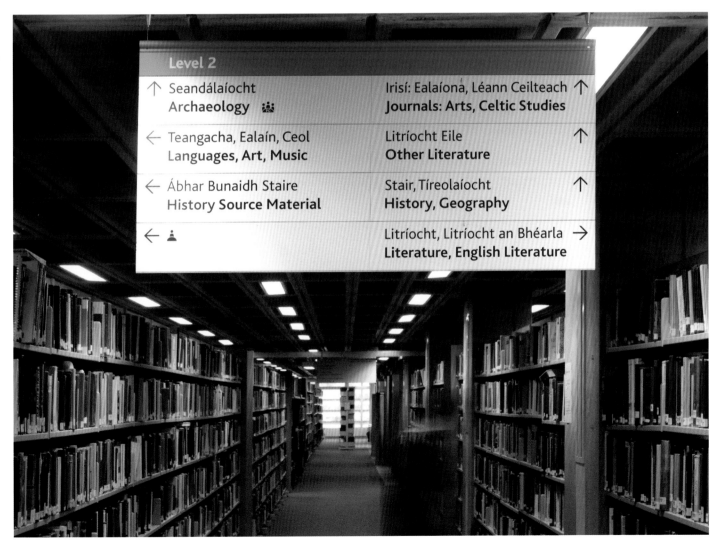

Level 2

↑ Seandálaíocht
Archaeology

Irisí: Ealaíona, Léann Ceilteach ↑
Journals: Arts, Celtic Studies

← Teangacha, Ealaín, Ceol
Languages, Art, Music

Litríocht Eile
Other Literature ↑

← Ábhar Bunaidh Staire
History **Source Material**

Stair, Tíreolaíocht
History, Geography ↑

← 🚧

Litríocht, Litríocht an Bhéarla →
Literature, English Literature

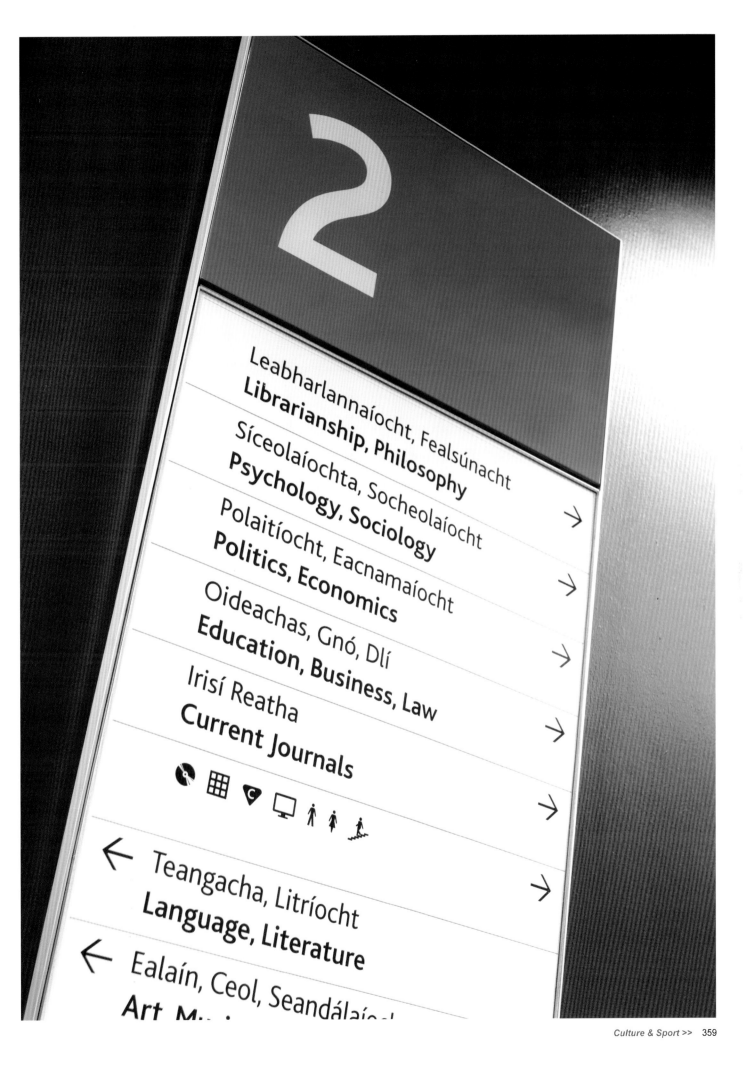

2

Leabharlannaíocht, Fealsúnacht
Librarianship, Philosophy

Síceolaíochta, Socheolaíocht
Psychology, Sociology →

Polaitíocht, Eacnamaíocht
Politics, Economics →

Oideachas, Gnó, Dlí
Education, Business, Law →

Irisí Reatha
Current Journals →

→

← Teangacha, Litríocht
Language, Literature →

← Ealaín, Ceol, Seandálaíocht
Art, Music

UCD
Business
School
Library >>

This former chapel, built in 1895, was converted into a library for the business school campus of University College Dublin. The design brief called for an understated, yet accessible, signage system to reflect the architectural heritage of the former chapel. One free-standing directory sign is the main information source for all subject categories shelved within the library. The colour palette is low-key, chosen to inform without distracting. The result is a striking, yet sophisticated, signage system that fits within the subtlety of its serene surroundings.

Design Agency:
BFK
Creative Directorr:
Aiden Kenny
Designer:
Marie Vahey
Client:
University College Dublin Library
Location:
Ireland
Date:
2008

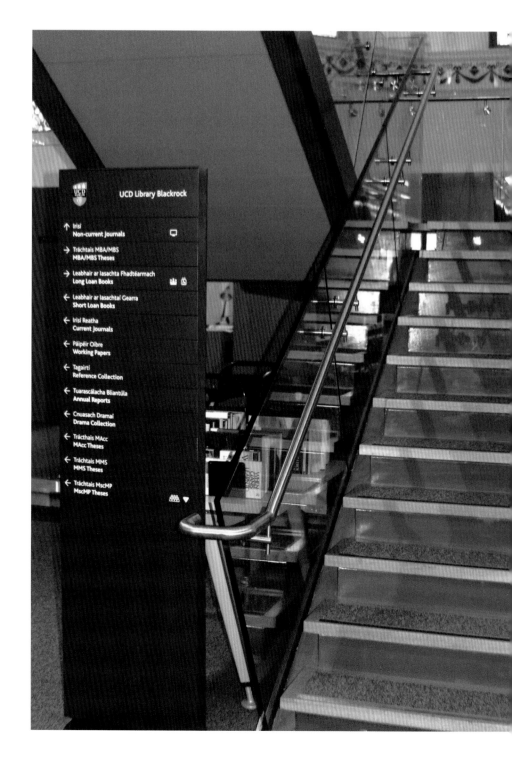

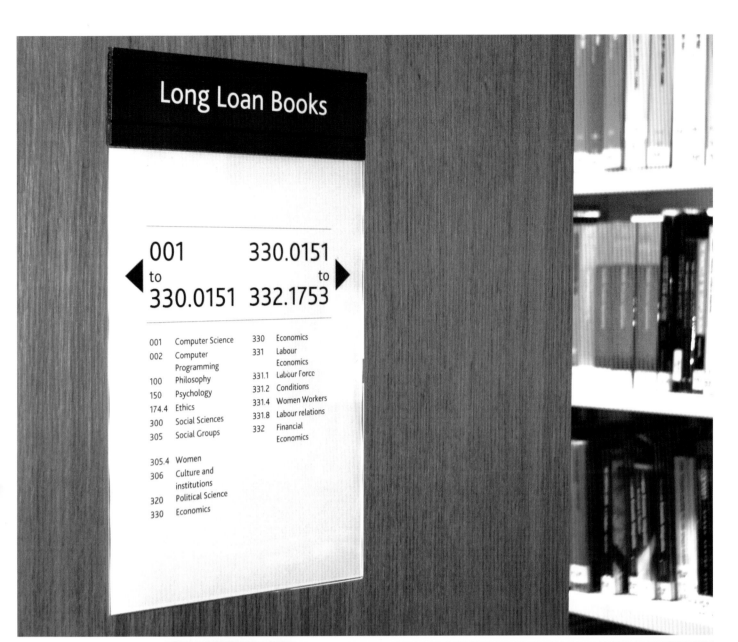

UCD Library Blackrock

↑ Irisí
Non-current Journals

→ Tráchtais MBA/MBS
MBA/MBS Theses

→ Leabhair ar Iasachta Fhadtéarmach
Long Loan Books

← Leabhair ar Iasachtaí Gearra
Short Loan Books

← Irisí Reatha
Current Journals

Scales —
Private
Cramming
School >>

It is a signage design for the private cramming school for children. The designer used the motif of measure and created a concept of signs, which can be described as "Measure that achieved growth". The scale is a flexible motif. The designer used learning tools that derive from measurements for the various signages. For example, he included the columns at the entrance, to resemble the scale of the nine size units (cm, yard, feet, inch, etc.). Children can learn unfamiliar scales by measuring their height. The designer created "Scales" as a contrivance where the design and space fuse with the measures.

Design Agency:
Nosigner
Client:
Takenaka Corporation
Location:
Japan
Date:
2009

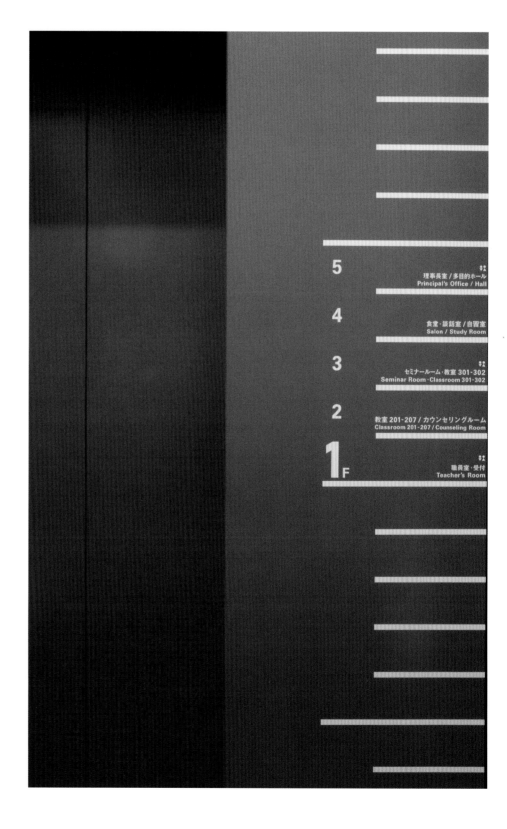

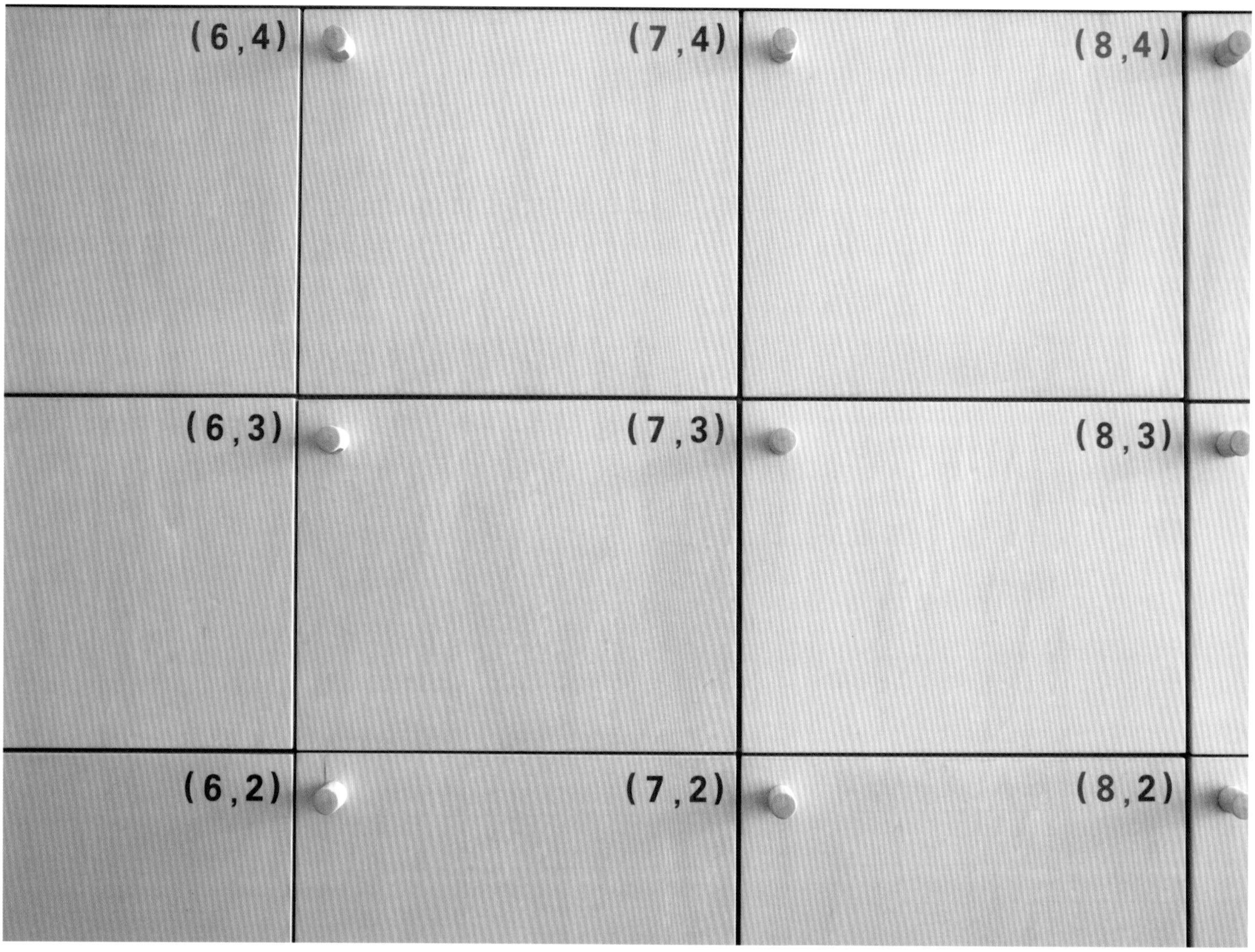
(6,4)
(7,4)
(8,4)
(6,3)
(7,3)
(8,3)
(6,2)
(7,2)
(8,2)

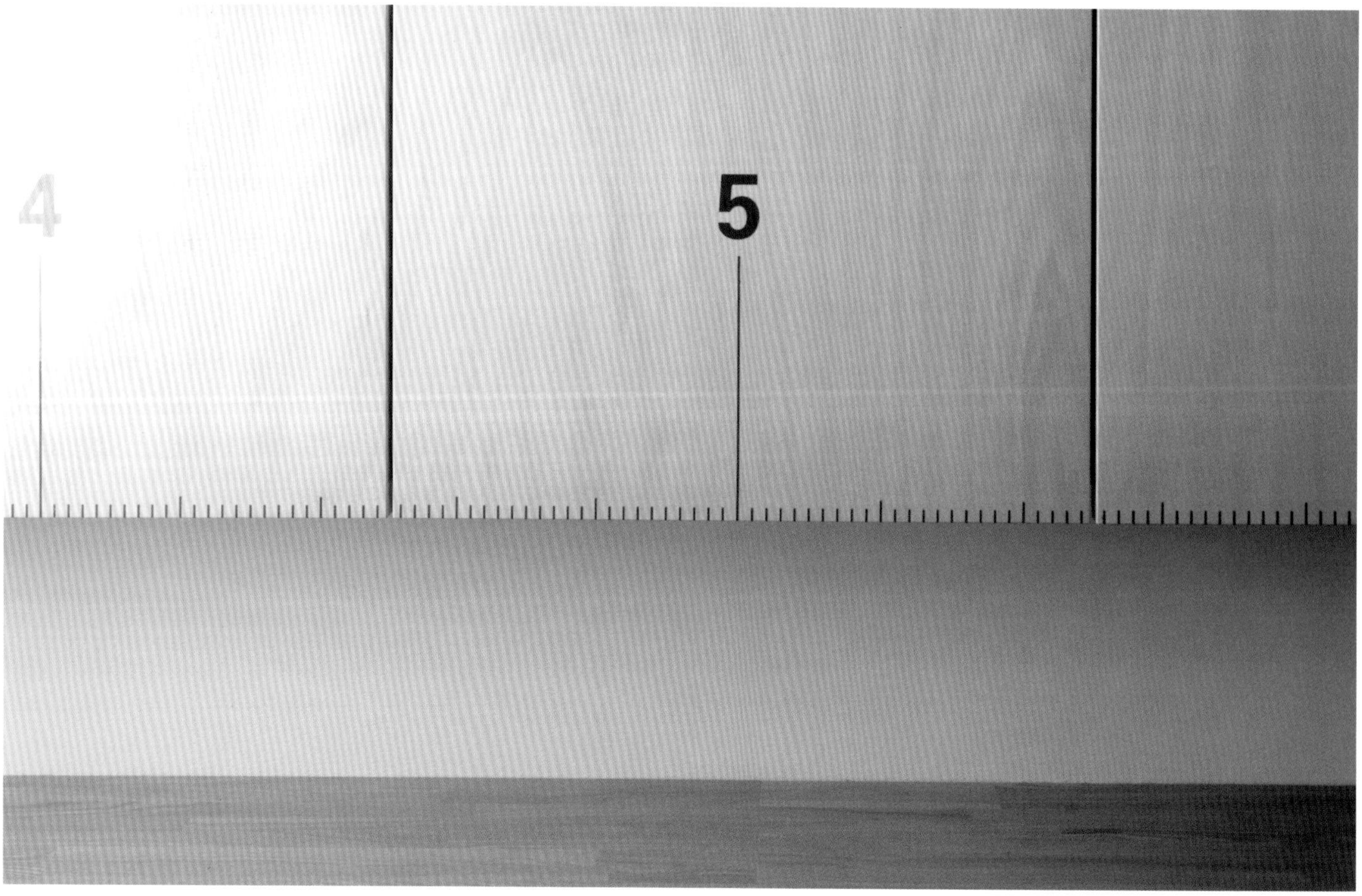
4
5

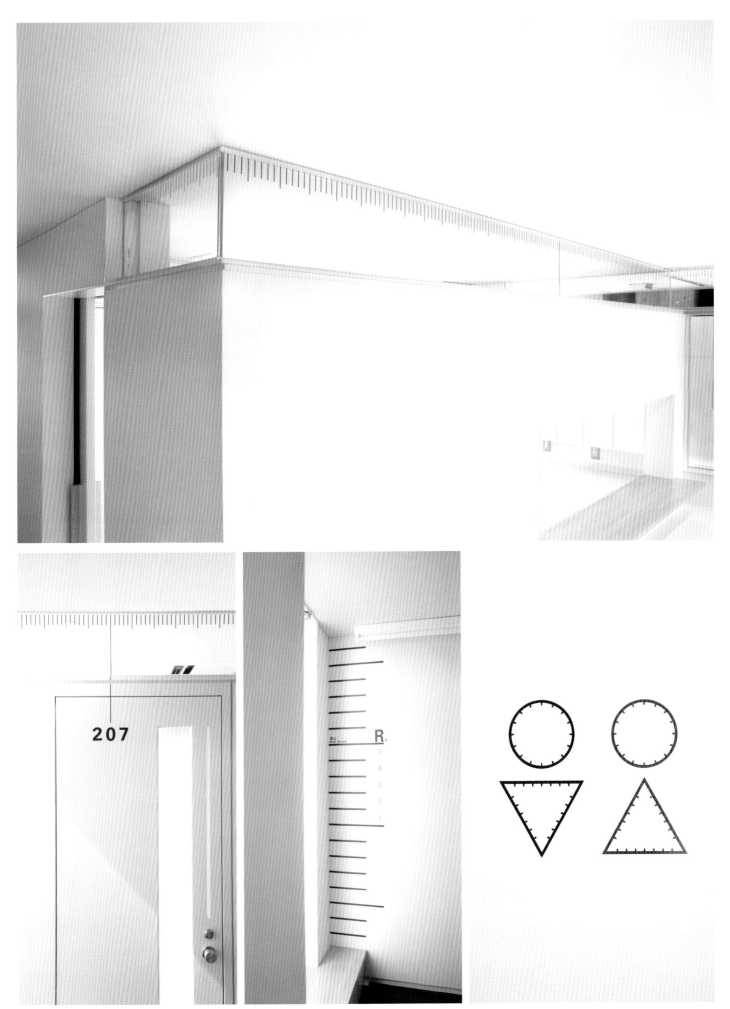

207

R_F

Miniature
Campus >>

This is a project for exhibiting the leading edge of the studies, at the Research Campus in the University of Tokyo, for public and business. There are two devices to achieve the goals of the project: the publication and finding business partners. The 60-metre-long map of the campus is drawn on of the building. The huge map drawn on the campus and the small handy map distributed for the visitors are related to each other. The studies at the laboratories located on the map are exhibited inside the 50cm x 50cm showcases. Moreover, the arrows using the shadow are placed everywhere in the campus. Therefore, they can easily guide to the laboratories. The drawn map on the building is the real miniature of the campus. The map is a primordial design of signage. The designer designed the graphic for the space to be an enlarged information map but smaller than the campus itself. Therefore he created a new "map" that has a double function. On the one hand it serves as an exhibition space for the different laboratory activities in the campus and on the other hand it works as a signage for the open campus.

Design Agency:
Nosigner
Client:
University of Tokyo Research Campus
Location:
Japan
Date:
2008

Yale
University >>

When Yale University embarked on a major redevelopment programme, Cooper, Robertson & Partners selected Two Twelve to assess the University's wayfinding and signage needs. Two Twelve designed a new system of signs and maps that meld a respect for 300-year-old traditions with contemporary simplicity and sensitivity to context.

Design Agency:
Two Twelve
Creative Director:
David Gibson
Designer:
Anthony Ferrara
Yanira Hernandez
Pamela Paul
Liz Reynolds
Dominic Borgia
Photography:
James Shanks
Client:
Yale University
Location:
USA
Date:
2007

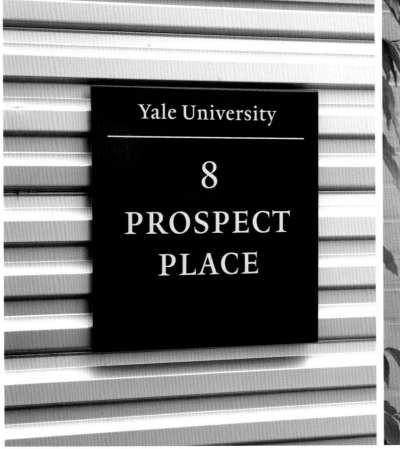

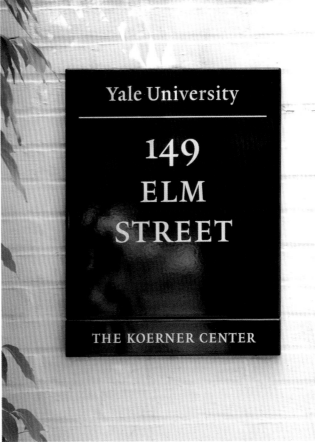

Panta
Rhei >>

In the design for the new accommodations of the public school Panta Rhei in Amstelveen, The Netherlands, there is a lot of attention on the balance between freedom and a sense of security. Snelder Architecten realised a building with many open multifunctional spaces where students can make themselves familiar with the teaching material. The interior design by i29 links up with that perfectly and gives the spaces an identity that connects with the students' environment and addresses them directly and personally. i29 let itself be inspired by the name of the school – Panta Rhei, meaning "everything flows", "everything is in motion". This led to a design that leaves space for the imagination of the users, offering elements that can be used flexibly, which also propagates the school's identity. Throughout the entire school poems have been applied to the linoleum floors and the furniture. The thought behind this is that there are moments outside of the classroom when you can learn and gain insights: often a casual setting is very inspiring. Over the neutral basis of tables and benches there is a fine fabric of black elements; consisting of the poems, the hassocks and the Magis One-chairs. The furniture is strong and robust, but does not look bulky, rather refined. Remarkable in this context is the choice of the Grcic chair. It matches well here because of its technical aura and it urges you to think about the design and production process. It is a vocational school after all. This is not a university, but it does not mean you do not have to challenge the students.

Design Agency:
i29 | snelder
Photography:
Jeroen Musch
Interior Builder:
Zwartwoud
Client:
Panta Rhei, Amstelveen
Location:
Amstelveen, The Netherlands
Date:
2010

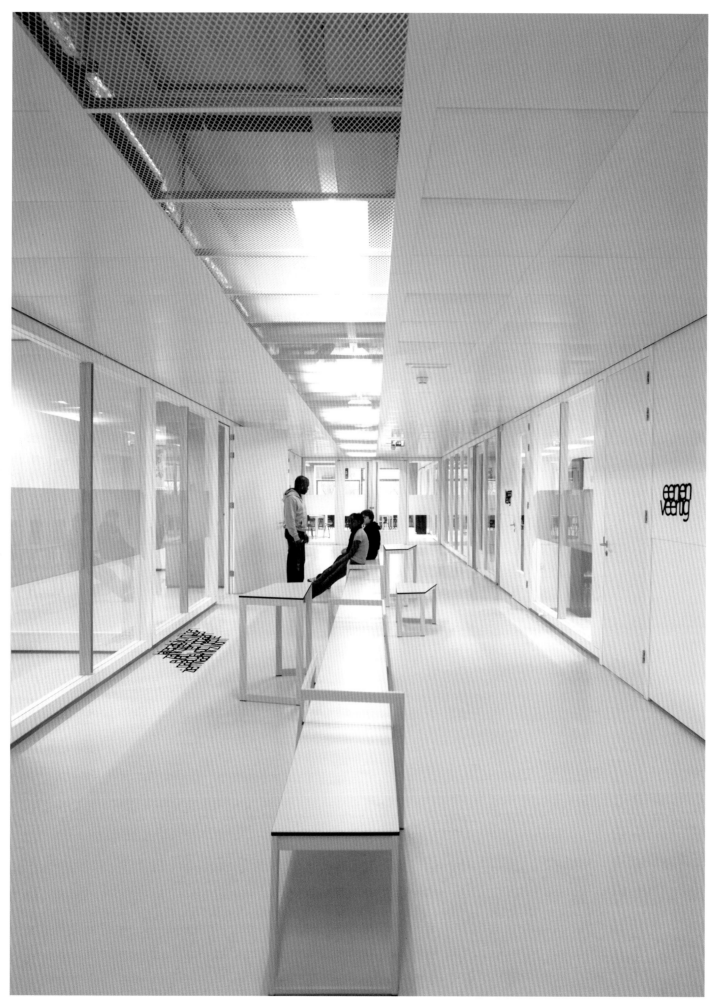

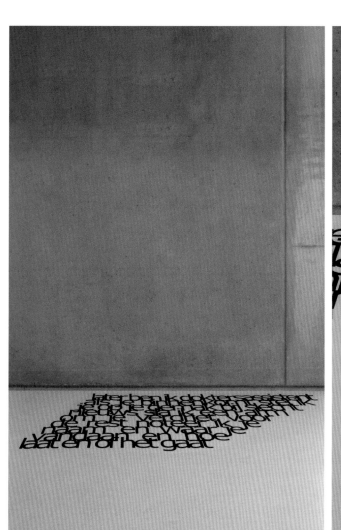

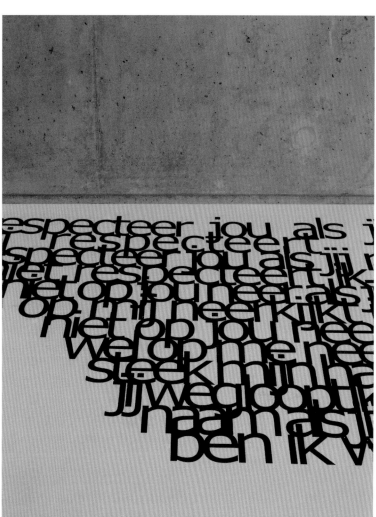

Tustin
Library >>

GNU Group worked closely with the project architect, Field Paoli, to design the sign programme for this new landmark building in the Orange County area of Los Angeles. Special branded graphics were developed to enrich the teen and children's areas of the library.

Design Agency:
GNU Group
Creative Director:
Tom Donnelly
Designer:
Darcy Belgarde
Photography:
Tom Donnelly
GKK Works:
Zwartwoud
Client:
Field Paoli Architects
Location:
USA
Date:
2009

Thurgau County Library >>

The website of the Thurgau County Library guides readers to go into the knowledge corridor of the Frauenfeld. The entrance to the library building is obvious. People through a clearly marked entrance can enter the library directly. The interior floor plan presents the layout of the rooms and space of the floor. The passages connecting various spaces are clearly marked and guide the reader towards specialised areas. The tags placed in a side way show the subject area, and lead out the vertically placed tags that mark the section and category. The database and table use the same vertically placed tags. The books and magazines of the free zones can be found out through a director query system. Data chain also runs here.

Design Agency:
Inform GmbH
Designer:
Richard Walter
Samuel Gäumann
Heinz Bothien
Emanuel Weissen
Client:
Kanton Thurgau in Frauenfeld
Location:
Switzerland
Date:
2008

600 Technik / 610 Medizin

610 Medizin

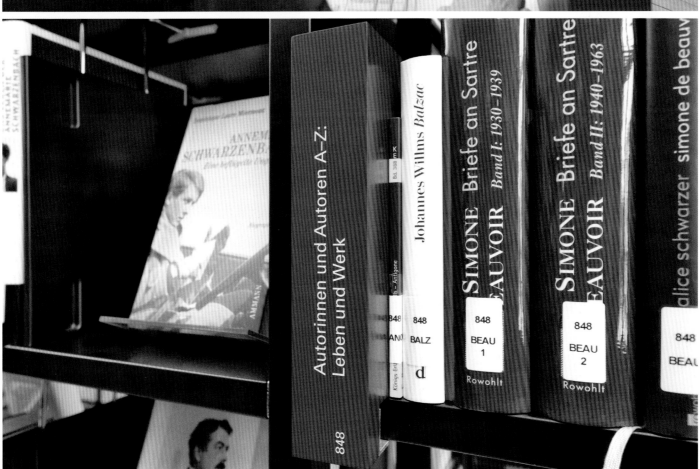

The
Rockefeller
University >>

The Rockefeller University is among the world's most respected medical research institutions. The campus is constantly undergoing renovation and over the coming years it will consist of state-of-the-art research facilities in a mix of contemporary and classic architecture. C&VE's signage programme serves as a unifying factor, respecting the existing, classical architecture by using traditional painted and oxidised bronze, but speaking to the contemporary buildings through simple forms and sans serif typography. The totem signs use opposing curved panels, resulting in slim structures with extreme rigidity, elegance, and good surface area. LED lighting concealed between the curved panels provides lighting for pathways.

Design Agency:
Calori & Vanden-Eynden / Design Consultants
Art Director:
David Vanden-Eynden
Designer:
David Vanden-Eynden
Ana Rosales-Boujnah
Photography:
Elliott Kaufman
Client:
Rockefeller University
Location:
USA
Date:
2009

Citi
Field >>

Two Twelve worked with the Mets and Populous architects to create a comprehensive environmental graphics programme for Citi Field, the New York Mets' new world-class ballpark. The extensive work includes the ballpark wayfinding signage and installations in the Jackie Robinson Rotunda, Citi Field's main entry.

Design Agency:
Two Twelve
Creative Director:
Anthony Ferrara
Jonathan Posnett
Designer:
Darlene van Uden, Vina Ayers, Michelle Cates,
Alexandria Lee, Maura Mathews, Corey Mintz,
Erik Murillo, Andy Ng, Nick Spriggs, Jennifer
Uchida, Dominic Borgia, and Laura Varacchi
Photography:
Christine Radecic
James Shanks
Client:
New York Mets Development Corporation
Location:
USA
Date:
2009

RIGHT FIELD
citi FIELD

FIELD LEVEL
107-130
RIGHT FIELD
Up to 301-325 | 401-414 501-514
Jackie Robinson Rotunda
Majestic Team Store
109
108

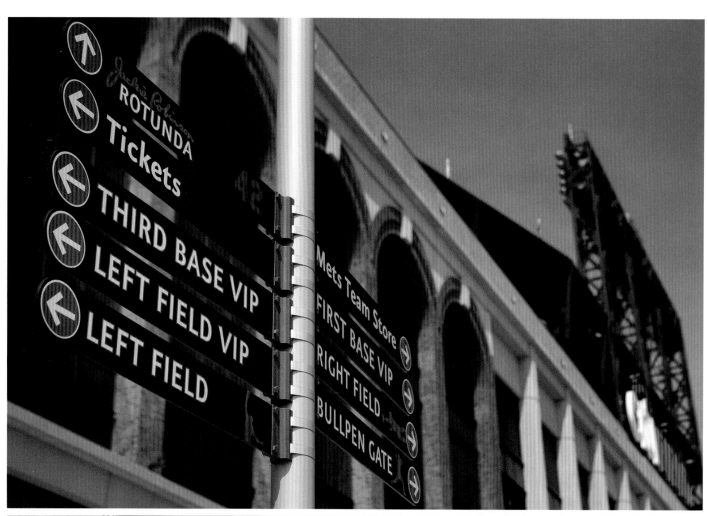

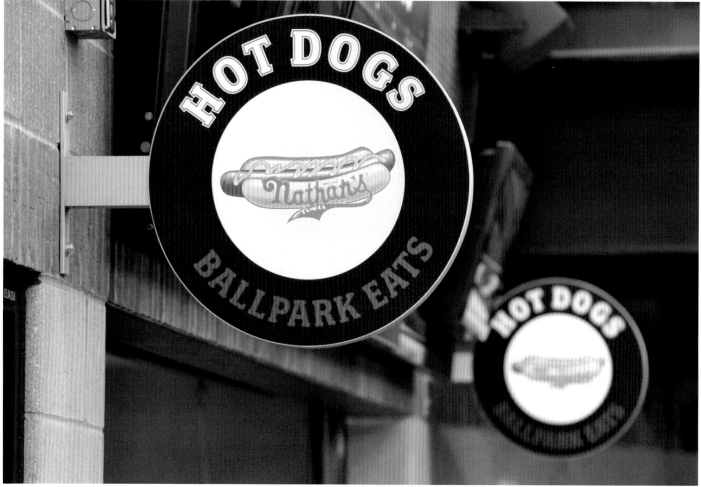

New
Meadow-
lands
Stadium >>

Two Twelve developed state-of-the-art graphics and wayfinding systems for the New Meadowlands Stadium, the new home of the New York Jets and New York Giants football teams. NMS is the only National Football League stadium shared by two teams. To make the venue feel like the "home field" for either team or other events, integral LED lighting in overhead signs can change colour.

Design Agency:
Two Twelve
Creative Director:
Ann Harakawa
Jonathan Posnett
Designer:
Darlene van Uden
Corey Mintz
Andy Ng
Project Partner:
Debra Magid Design
EwingCole
360 Architecture
Bruce Mau Design
Architectural Graphics Inc.
Photography:
Jonathan Posnett
Client:
New Meadowlands Stadium LLC
Location:
USA
Date:
2010

Twickenham
Stadium >>

Twickenham Stadium is the largest dedicated, and one of the most impressive, rugby stadiums in the world.

The stadium has undergone an £80 million redevelopment to rebuild the South Stand. The new Stand includes a four-star hotel, a Virgin Active health and fitness club, a Marriott hotel, banqueting facilities, conference facilities and a theatre.

The challenge was to position the venue as a destination identity in its own right, a place for entertainment, conferences, and business meetings and of course rugby.

As a part of the re-branding the designers have designed a new wayfinding strategy for the entire stadium complex, both inside and outside the ground, including the route from the railway station, road signs, building signage, banners, environmental graphics, information zones and seating zones.

Design Agency:
Hat-trick
Creative Director:
Gareth Howat
Jim Sutherland
Designer:
Gareth Howat
Jim Sutherland
Adam Giles
Richard Conn
Client:
Twickenham Stadium
Location:
Twickenham, UK
Date:
2008

Yankee
Stadium >>

After being selected in a national competition, the firm, in collaboration with architects Populous, designed all stadium graphics, sign systems, sculptural and media installations, and retail systems for the new Yankee Stadium, one of the largest and most complex sports venues in the United States.

Yankee Stadium's wayfinding programme encompasses over 3,000 signs, from the monolithic rear-illuminated lettering atop the scoreboard and ceremonial Gate 4 façade, to minimalist, back-of-house wayfinding. The lettering used on the larger signs and v-incised into the limestone façade duplicate the font depicted on archival photographs of the 1923 stadium. The New York Yankees' pinstripes, interlocking NY logo and signature navy blue are used to infuse the team's image throughout the Stadium. The sign programme has been crafted with stainless steel, porcelain enamel and elegant typography in manner appropriate for Yankee Stadium – a place that has always been far more than just a ballpark.

Design Agency:
C&G Partners
Partner-in-Charge and Project Manager:
Keith Helmetag
Associate Partner and Lead Sign Designer:
Amy Siegel
Graphic Designer:
Craig Gephart
Sign Architect:
Mika Owens
Photography:
Chuck Choi
Brandon Downing
Craig Gephart
Client:
The New York Yankees
Location:
USA
Date:
2009

The
New York
Jets Training
Centre >>

Pentagram has worked with the Jets since 2002 on the development of its graphic identity, including the design of a custom typeface called Jets Bold designed by Hoefler & Frere-Jones that is used in all of the team's communications. The graphics have become part of the team DNA, and at the training centre they are integrated into the architecture to extend the team's identity into the space. Jets Bold appears throughout the building: in supergraphic slogans from inspirational speeches by coaches that appear on the walls; in abstracted patterns in stairwells; on the team's own Wall of Fame, named for 1999 MVP Curtis Martin; and on the nameplates for the players' lockers.

The players' level is centred on a long hallway that functions as a spine or axis that connects the various operations of the team: rooms devoted to education, health and fitness, including an auditorium for coaching, a classroom for teaching game plays, and a gym and weight room. The portals to these areas are identified by dimensional signage of the words "Learn", "Coach" and "Train," all set in Jets Bold. One side of the players' hallway looks out onto the field; the other side features a 146-metre-long mural of fans in the stands at a Jets game, the image players pass by just before they hit the field.

Design Agency:
Pentagram Design
Art Director:
Michael Gericke
Designer:
Michael Gericke
Don Bilodeau
Jed Skillins
Client:
New York Jets
Location:
USA
Date:
2010

Falls Creek
Alpine
Ski Resort>>

The Falls Creek Alpine Resort required the development of a wayfinding system to help visitors navigate the complex ski resort. A modular system of sign types was created to provide information in a wide variety of directions to suit the complex village layout and changing seasonal functions. The design of the sign system aims to promote the highest possible visibility of information whilst retaining the smallest presence of supporting structure. The system is extremely efficient, using a minimum number of elements for a range of sign types, whilst also minimising the production energy requirements. The materials and finishes have been developed to withstand the freeze/thaw conditions and abuse from skiiers, snow transport and the harsh alpine environment.

Design Agency:
Buro North
Designer:
Soren Luckins
Tom Allnutt
Dave Williamson
Photography:
Peter Bennetts
Client:
Falls Creek Resort Management
Location:
Australia
Date:
2010

Moreton
Bay
Cycleway >>

The 150-kilometre-long Moreton Bay Cycleway (MBC) is the longest planned cycle route on Australia's east. The MBC will not only assist regular cyclists and commuters, it will also be part of a wider tourism campaign for Moreton Bay promoting greater recreation such as cycling trips to nearby islands. The brief was to develop a simple, cost effective sign system that could be rolled out over time. The signage system was intended to clearly identify the cycleway and then provide information and advice for cyclists travelling on the cycleway. The signage would give all visitors a sense of confidence when travelling and assist with public safety and security. The designers have developed a simple "Kit of Signs" that can be applied as specific sections of the MBC are completed. The signs, strength is in their use of a simple identifier, use of colour in the landscape as well as detailed information tailored to meet the needs of the cyclists.

Design Agency:
Dot Dash
Designer:
Heath Pedrola
Photography:
Heath Pedrola
Client:
Moreton Bay Regional Council
Location:
Australia
Date:
2007

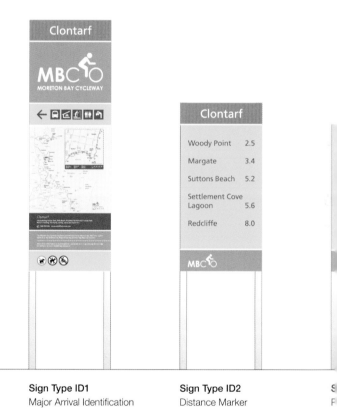

Sign Type ID1
Major Arrival Identification

Sign Type ID2
Distance Marker

MORETON BAY CYCLEWAY

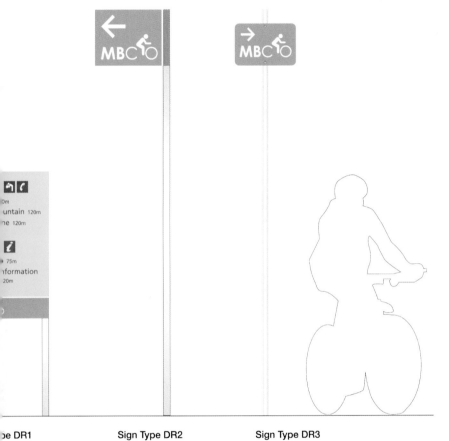

be DR1
ervices Directional

Sign Type DR2
Pathway Flag Directional

Sign Type DR3
On-road Route Directional

Sign Type ID3
Pathway Surface Identification

Sign types within the sign family are intended to work together to address all possible configurations of cycleway including on road, off road, and shared paths.

Signage identifies the cycleway (promoting brand) and provides the necessary information and advice for effective use of the cycleway by all visitors.

ID1
To identify major arrival and departure points along the cycleway. Directs to local area public services and facilities. Provides mapping and local shire tourist information. Provides regulatory information for relative section of cycleway.

ID2
To provide journey distance information. Distance makers to be in kilometres and relevant to the local area. Distance makers for each sign to show journey to the north and the south along cycleway.

ID3
To provide identification on the cycleway path. Can also be used as a directional tool typically where the cycleway path joins or crosses other paths and roads.

DR1
To direct cyclists and pedestrians to local public services and facilities. Public services and facilities shown on the signs are to be within close proximity of the cycleway.

DR2
To direct cyclists at major decision points on the cycleway. Typically where the cycleway path joins or crosses other paths and roads.

DR3
To be used in conjunction with traffic signs for on-road sections of the cycleway to direct and identify the route.

4.1

INDEX >>

Kontrapunkt >>

W: http://www.kontrapunkt.com/
T: + 45 3393 1883
P: 322

Lebowitz|Gould|Design, Inc. >>

W: http://www.lgd-inc.com/
T: 212.695.5700
P: 222, 284

Meuser Architekten GmbH >>

W: http://www.meuser-architekten.de/
T: +49.30.20 69 69 20
P: 180, 192

Moniteurs GmbH >>

W: http://www.moniteurs.de/
T: +49 0 30 24 3456 0
P: 058

Naroska Design >>

W: http://www.naroska.de/
T: +49 30 28091991
P: 202

Nicolas Vrignaud >>

W: http://www.b-headroom.com/
T: +33 6 61 53 17 74
P: 274

Nosigner >>

W: http://www.nosigner.com/
T: 81(0) 3 5834 7652
P: 364

P-06 Atelier >>

W: http://www.p-06-atelier.pt/
T: 00351 213 011 834
P: 156, 250, 306

Paprika studio >>

W: http://paprika.com/
T: 515 276 6000
P: 086

PearsonLloyd >>

W: http://www.pearsonlloyd.com/
T: 44(0) 20 7033 4440
P: 082, 168

Pentagram >>

W: http://www.pentagram.com/
T: +44 (0)20 7229 3477
P: 234, 340, 416

R2 >>

W: http://www.r2design.pt/
T: +351 22 938 68 65
P: 318

RTKL Associates Inc. >>

W: http://www.rtkl.com/
T: + 44 (0)20 7306 0404
P: 014, 242

Shakespear SRL >>

W: www.shakespearweb.com
T: +54 11 4836 1333
P: 062, 134

Square Peg Design >>

W: http://www.sqpeg.com/
T: 510 596 8814
P: 128, 258

Sussman/Prejza & Co., Inc. >>

W: http://www.sussmanprejza.com/
T: 310 836 3939
P: 172, 254

Tassinari/Vetta >>

W: http://www.tassinarivetta.it/
T: +39 040 3498206
P: 288

Thonik >>

W: http://www.thonik.com/
T: +31 20 468 3525
P: 048

Two Twelve >>

W: http://www.twotwelve.com/
T: 212 254/6670
P: 106, 372, 398, 402

Visual Communications, Inc. >>

W: http://www.vciexhibits.com/
T: 880 487 5964
P: 174

Vista System >>

W: http://www.vistasystem.com/
T: 800 468-4782
P: 178

©2010 by Design Media Publishing Limited
This edition published in May 2011

Design Media Publishing Limited
20/F Manulife Tower
169 Electric Rd, North Point
Hong Kong
Tel: 00852-28672587
Fax: 00852-25050411
E-mail: Kevinchoy@designmediahk.com
www.designmediahk.com

Editing: Jie Zhou, Muzi Guan, Zhe Gao & Liying Wang
Proofreading: Catherine Chang
Cover Design: Muzi Guan
Design/Layout: Jie Zhou

ISBN 978-988-19739-3-1

Printed in China